I am HUNGRY *to Know* HOW TO LIVE

*Does Your Worldview Truly Satisfy
All Your Most Burning Questions?*

"He satisfies the longing soul, and   Psalm   BBH
fills the hungry soul with goodness." 107:9

B. BARROW HAMBY

I Am Hungry to Know How to Live

Copyright © 2018 by B. Barrow Hamby. All rights reserved. No portion of this book may be reproduced, stored in a retrieval system, or transmitted in any form or by any means, except for brief quotations in printed reviews, without prior permission of B. Barrow Hamby. Requests may be submitted by email: bebar@powerc.net.

ISBN 978-0-9899103-3-0

Scriptures taken from Amplified Bible. Copyright © 1965 by Zondervan Publishing House. Used by permission. All rights reserved.

Scripture marked NKJV taken from the New King James Version®. Copyright © 1982 by Thomas Nelson. Used by permission. All rights reserved.

Scriptures marked KJV taken from King James Version. Public Domain.

Indulgence asked for any failure on our part to reach any holder of copyrighted selections.

Editing, cover design, and page formatting by ChristianEditingServices.com

Table of Contents

Section 3: The Journey Onward

Preface

*E*very thoughtful human being inevitably asks questions as he observes life around him. Mankind broods over the problems, losses and sorrows, injustices and tragedies of human existence—and often despairs, stricken at heart at being unable to interpret it all.

Trying to explain the baffling mystery, people throughout history have come up with countless worldviews. I propose that fundamentally there are only two worldviews—either this world is all there is to reality—or it is not all there is.

The one view claims this cosmos—this earth and all that the life lived here entails—is simply "it." There is purportedly nothing outside the cosmos. We simply explain the present world based on this world itself (and on the operation of chance). Supposedly everything in the cosmos is part of and influenced by everything else in it—and is thereby self-explanatory (explains itself). Resultantly, there are no purpose and no goal in existence. It "just happened." And there is no progress because everything is on an endless cycle—both coming from and going nowhere. We ourselves came from nothing and go to nothing. We're born, we live, we die. Good-bye.

Or is there something beyond this cosmos? The biblical worldview believes there is a Designer of this cosmos, an intelligent Creator who is outside of and transcends His creation. This worldview submits for consideration that the Creator of this world can provide the explanation for the cosmos as it is. The Bible asserts that God had a purpose in making this world and us. It instructs that mankind, as the apex of His creation, is created in His image—and as such, designed with the intention of sharing His character and fellowship with Him forever. Additionally, this Creator can reveal to the questioning mind: *This is where you started,* and *this is where you're going.*

Every intelligent person finds four questions that press upon him begging for answers.

How did we come to be—and why? What went wrong? Is there any hope? and *How will it all end?*

With no belief in a sovereign God, modern materialism and the humanistic worldview (a man-centered ideology that includes a basic tenet that man is intrinsically good) maintain that humanity's existence as a whole is the result of a fortuitous accident. It considers the origin of the universe as impossible to explain (most likely merely the result of a long, complex evolution). It asserts that since this life is all that we have scientific knowledge of, it is up to us humans to solve the world's problems, define what is right and wrong, and give meaning and purpose to life through human love and natural reason. This worldview gives political, sociologic, economic, or psychological explanations for "what's gone wrong" with life—and thus the adherent's answers for any hope must come from human efforts to find solutions in those respective fields.

It cannot offer any adequate accounting for why evil exists but lamely suggests it is just all "part of the way things are." A classic example of a solution according to a godless worldview is Marxist communism, which concluded "the" problem was social inequality—and if everyone were forcibly made equal then evil would disappear. Obviously, it has not. Significantly, many atheists (perhaps some of the most intelligent atheists—and likely the more honest atheists) admit that the primary reason they choose not to believe there is a God is that they do not want there to be a God. They simply do not want to be accountable to anyone other than themselves—especially to an unseen Creator who intrudes upon their morality. A worldview denying the existence of a God is more comfortable for some people—at least temporarily.

In contrast, a biblical (and Christian) worldview answers the question of how we (and the world we live in) came to be in terms of the doctrine of creation. "In the beginning God created . . ." (Genesis 1:1 NKJV)—and everything follows from that. It teaches that God made the world good but that one of His creatures fell and became the catalyst for a decision by the first human beings that damaged our world. Intentional human sin (rebellion of the creature against the Creator) brought consequences against mankind and onto the earth itself that are not in themselves definable as good. Yes, we all know things are not as we would want them to be or as they ought to be. Earthquakes, injustice, infectious disease, a child's cry, tumors, venomous snakes, famine, cruelty of man against man—none of this was intended by God. The biblical worldview believes everything wrong is ultimately traceable to human sin. The righteous wrath and judgment of our Creator is the cosmic consequence of our choice to rebel against His authority (not trusting His goodwill toward us)—and ultimately our rejecting Him.

Is there, then, any hope? There is only one worldview that accurately reveals mankind's true problem—and its only real answer. If left to ourselves, there is no hope. But in the gospel (good news) of Jesus Christ there is absolute hope. "But God shows *and* clearly proves His [own] love for us by the fact that while we were still sinners Christ, the Messiah, the Anointed One, died for us" (Romans 5:8). Our hope as inveterate rebels against our Maker is that God Himself made a way for us to return to His favor. He sent His own Son to our earth. Jesus took on human nature to be as one of us—and as man, He took upon Himself the guilt of mankind's sin (as well as the punishment of separation from our Maker we had brought on ourselves).

So where is human history headed? One worldview predicts our annihilation. The Bible, however, teaches that it concludes with the kingdom of Christ on earth—where the righteousness and justice of a good God will be applied under the lordship of Jesus, mankind's Redeemer. It also promises a new heaven and a new earth where believers in Jesus (as the atonement for their sin) will no longer experience tears, pain, or sorrow; where the lame will leap, the blind will see, and where all that is wrong will be made right. Notably, this worldview also includes the very real threat of hell— eternal separation from God (from our very source of life, most significantly the eternal life of our spirits)—for some people.

Undoubtedly there remain many mysteries in life. Even as believers in a caring God, when sorrow intrudes into our lives, the mystery of unanswerable questions can edge us toward despair. And yet, the whole universe teems with mystery. It is recorded in history that long ago a man named Job suffered more tragedy in his life than any one man could seem possibly able to bear. But God drew near this agonizingly afflicted and deeply perplexed soul, and asked him a searching question: "Where were you when I laid the foundations of the earth?" (Job 38:4 NKJV). By this he prodded Job to realize that mysteries equally insoluble as his own life's problems were all around him—above his head and under his feet. God pointed out to Job man himself cannot explain the creation of the world; he cannot fully understand the light and darkness, places where the storehouses are of wind and snow, the essence of storms, the influence of sunshine, or the instincts of animals. Mysteries all.

Should we then be surprised if we find that in God's dealings with us human beings, many times we will not find our questions answered? "For My thoughts *are* not your thoughts, Nor *are* your ways My ways," says the Lord. For *as* the heavens are higher than the earth, So are My ways higher than your ways, And My thoughts than your thoughts" (Isaiah 55:8–

9 NKJV). God, our Maker, has the right to choose not to answer all our questions. Secondarily, we are not capable of understanding all His ways and reasons—any more than a very young child can comprehend the mysteries of human life. But what God does want us to know is that we are infinitely dear and valuable to Him, and behind all the mystery is a Father's heart beating in love for His children. Jesus told His cherished disciples, "I still have many things to say to you, but you cannot bear *them* now" (John 16:12 NKJV). And He said to Peter, "You do not understand now what I am doing, but you will understand later on" (John 13:7).

May you hear that same kind voice pleading, "Trust me"—and "Let not your heart be troubled, neither let it be afraid" (John 14:27 NKJV). I invite you, reader, to come with me and explore in these pages this great Lover of your soul's unchanging love, and to trust Him—even when you cannot yet see or fully understand.

SECTION I

The Search for the Gate

Chapter 1

I Am Hungry

I am hungry, and I cannot find bread that satisfies. I have tried many different kinds of "bread"...

I tried the bread of pleasure and entertainment, one round after another, but the brief satisfaction evaporated like the dew. I tried art, music, literature, and the supposedly high things of culture, but I found no lasting satisfaction there. I tried the bread of work worthy in the eyes of men and hoped accomplishment would win an identity for me that would meet my need, but none of that satisfied any longer. I thought surely the bread of wealth would assuage my hunger, but material possessions and a comfortable lifestyle left me still wanting something—something else. I tried the bread of philosophy, studying human nature and all angles of the issues and problems of life, debating and discussing, and discussing and debating in never-ending circles. I could find in philosophy no peace.

I tried communing with nature and sought bread in the beauty of creation. I wandered by the seashores and climbed the mountains, asking, "Is it there, is it there?" But my voice only cried back at me in long, hollow echoes, and I hungered still. Surely human fellowship—love relationships, the joys of family life—would make me whole, I reasoned. But even that, even the best it could offer, was not enough. I tried the bread of social service, of being a "good person," giving of my time and energy to meet mankind's needs, but all my good deeds left me still empty. Perhaps change would feed me. That's it! I at length concluded. A new environment, a new situation— I'll quit my job, I'll move to a new town, I'll break out of this marriage and try a fresh start with someone else. Or maybe following these new ideas and views about life's purpose and these innovative breakthroughs—a revolution altogether— surely that would produce paradise for me. And yet . . .

So many messages pounding at the door of my mind, all promising satisfaction. Yet all these "breads" could only go so far—and no farther—to assuage my soul-hunger. That nameless inner longing remains.

Is this your experience? We are all looking for certain things. Where are peace, joy, happiness, security, significance? Where is life in a very real sense worthy of the name?

Many centuries ago a powerful king, renowned throughout the world for his wisdom, wrote a lengthy treatise resulting from his own personal quest for value. He had determined to seek until he discovered what is of real value in life, and he had all the resources available for his search any human being could possibly desire. He wrote in descriptive detail about the myriad avenues "under the sun" proposed by humanity throughout its history for pursuing significance in life.

After long years of the most diligent searching for some fixed unchanging value that could serve as a proper basis for living, that great seeker felt all his efforts had been like "grasping for wind'—it was all elusive, transitory, fleeting. The Preacher, as he called himself when he compiled his conclusions, could not, after all, claim to have discovered the answer for which he had sought, but he wrote a very telling statement. He succinctly concluded that the whole duty of man is reverence for God and obeying Him (see Ecclesiastes 12:13).

The very wise man had not found the certainty he yearned for "under the sun"—that is, on this earth, in this life. He was compelled by his observations, therefore, to seek the value he longed for "above the sun," so to speak.

Centuries later, another great searcher expressed the opinion that the modern world had "lost God" and that without Him, it couldn't live. It seemed prophetic. We are a world that has lost God—and we are a broken, bleeding world. Mankind has chosen to go it alone, without God. We find self-sufficiency a better way, a more attractive way—and so the independent human race leaves out God. And because it leaves out God, its Creator, all this choice can essentially offer is a mirage.

My life is a journey. You and I are on a pilgrimage; we are sojourners. We entered this world, began this journey, and we're all heading toward a destination. We do not need to travel very far along before the rose-colored glasses we may have started off with do not work anymore. We begin to see that life has difficulties along the way—and soon enough we grow tired. We look around in this desert, hoping to find water to refresh us, and, thankfully, we see in the distance what appears to be a supply. Ah, over there! But when we finally arrive "there," we find no water—no water at all. It is just an illusion shimmering in the sands. Over and over the hopeful thing that seems close enough to grasp eludes us, escapes us. How long can we go on and on and on, thus bewildered (and mocked and deluded by mirages)?

The stark and immutable reality is that nothing less than God Himself can fill our hungry souls—for the soul's capacity was designed by God for Himself. My soul belongs to God, my Maker. He alone can satisfy.

If I am at long last realizing that all my efforts to find the meaning I have so long sought have resulted in absolute futility—that I remain empty (and as desperately so as a pauper), then I may be on the verge of a most momentous threshold! I just may have found the gate, the entrance, to the life I so achingly seek.

Nestled in Our Cravings

*D*oes your heart yearningly inquire, "How then, do I live?" Does your aching mind plead, "Won't someone tell me? Is there no one who can give me a key?" Friend, I encourage you to ponder this thought: an answer lies nestled in our very cravings.

We are the work of God's hands. It is written that He has planted eternity in men's hearts (see Ecclesiastes 3:11). I myself cannot believe that He would have created desires within us, longings to reach the Infinite, merely to tantalize. Such a possibility does not fit the nature of the Father I know.

It is He Himself who has given us life. Will He not also give us all we need for living the life He intended when He created us? The very gift of the one promises the gift of the other. Our hunger to know how to live, then, is implanted by God, our Maker. Has He implanted a hunger that He will not satisfy?

A Sense of Lack

Our minds are restless because our God-given intellects seek a purpose. We seek a purpose beyond the pleasure of the moment. We seek a purpose beyond even a lifetime. There exists within us all a divinely instilled sense of purpose that reaches through the ages—which nothing under the sun can satisfy. Is there any hope of finding that purpose?

Let us observe the contrast between two men of whom the Master spoke. One man was a Pharisee, a learned man whose strict observance of certain practices gave him confidence that he was a righteous man; the other man was a tax collector, a profession that was often considered synonymous with cheating (see Luke 18:9–14).

They both happened to be at the same place at the same time. They were in a temple, so that tells us they were both "in the same place" in another sense: they were each seeking satisfaction, desiring to assuage their inner hunger for that "something beyond" what their day-to-day lives brought them. No doubt, in some way, they both wanted to establish that connection with their real purpose in existence.

Their methods of seeking satisfaction, however, were profoundly different. And perhaps we will see that that foundation made all the difference in their hope of finding.

One was a religious man—that is, a man who did all the right things outwardly to be a "good person" and felt rather smugly that he had made considerable progress in moral attainment. The other man knew better than to think any such thing of himself. He had no victories to show over issues in his life that regularly pricked his conscience. But he did have a hunger for victory.

One man was quite self-satisfied; the other was dissatisfied. One man was full of presumption and prideful assurance that he had earned right standing with God. The other man was humble, clearly recognizing his inability by his own efforts to be the man his conscience urged him to be. He was a man with a much more accurate view of himself before a holy God than the first man had.

The Master stated clearly that only one of the two men found what he was looking for. The boastful sense of possession left the one man empty, while the penitent sense of want sent the other man away full (see Luke 18:9–14). Could it be, then, it is our very sense of lack that is the measure of our hope?

The Promise Indicates a Well

Well over a million people were there—with no water. Can you imagine yourself among the Israelites there in the desert? They desperately needed water! Did the Lord lead them out of Egypt to make them die of thirst? Would He mock their trust in Him?

No! He pledged Himself to give all they required. He promised them water. "That is the well of which the Lord had said to Moses, Assemble the people together, and I will give them water" (Numbers 21:16). You see, friend, the promise of a well meant there was a well. And sure enough, there in the barren, bleak desert, a well sprang up—and their thirst was abundantly quenched.

We too are thirsting. We need fresh supplies for the life of our souls. Has God promised to give, to meet our needs? Yes, of course—again and again in His Word. Thus, the promise is itself an indication of the provision. Our Creator will not cheat His creature who trusts in Him—who depends upon His truth, depends on His being true to His word. The heavenly Father will not break his word to His child. Abraham was fully satisfied and assured that God was able and mighty to keep His word and to do what He had promised (see Romans 4:21). We can indeed be absolutely certain that whatever promise He has bound Himself by, He is able also to make good.

Therefore, like David, we can plead, "Remember the word to Your servant, Upon which You have caused me to hope" (Psalm 119:49 NKJV). This is a most blessed key to prevailing prayer. Charles Spurgeon wrote, "It is a double argument. First, it is Your Word—will You not keep it? [Why have You spoken it, if You will not make it good?] And secondly, You have caused me to hope in it. [Will You disappoint the hope which You Yourself have birthed in me?]"[1] Since our gracious God has promised to provide for us, let us be encouraged to look for the wells.

Yet may we also realize that along with our God, we too have a part to play. Regarding the miraculous springing up of water the Lord caused in the desert, we read that it was "dug by the nation's nobles" (Numbers 21:18 NKJV). We too must dig. God doesn't reward the idle! We must seek after what He has promised to give. Notably also, while the leaders dug, simultaneously the people of Israel sang—they praised God in song. And likewise for us today (in our "deserts"), when our thanksgiving to God evidences our trust in His faithfulness,

---

1   Mrs. Charles E. Cowman, *Streams in the Desert*, Volume 1. (Zondervan Publishing House, 1965), 75.

our praise can still open previously undetected fountains of His blessing and provision (see Isaiah 44:3). Desire, effort, and faith must be active to open the channels for His grace to flow to us. As we fervently seek Him, we will surely discover His wells of water—living water. "They shall not hunger or thirst . . . for He Who has mercy on them will lead them, and by the springs of water will He guide them" (Isaiah 49:10).

Now, Lord, let the word which You have spoken be established, and do as You have said, that Your name (nature, character) may be magnified forever (see 1 Chronicles 17: 23–24). Thus, when we feel led to put our finger on a promise of Scripture (under the confident impression that God Himself is speaking its message to us personally), we can in utter faith take the strong position of humbly pleading this reasonable request: "Do as Thou hast said." Importantly, however, we must be sure of one thing: that we are in the line of God's purpose. Just as David expressed in Psalm 119:49, it is essential that we be fully persuaded that what we ask is in accordance with God's will. Many times we may ask for things that are not absolutely promised—and though we persevere in our petitioning, we wonder why the answer does not come. The problem is not in God as the promise-maker and the promise-keeper but rather in the nature of our asking. When our petitions are aligned with our Father's will, we can have confidence that He hears— and will answer. F. B. Meyer wrote, "There need be no anguish, or struggle, or wrestling; we simply present the check, and ask for cash, produce the promise, and claim its fulfillment; nor can there be any doubt as to its issue."[2]

Human promises are often worthless, and many a broken

---

2   Ibid., 74.

promise has left a broken heart. Our loving Father's promises, however, are "exceedingly great and precious" (2 Peter 1:4 NKJV)—based on the everlasting faithfulness of God. Since the world began, God has not broken a single one of His promises to those who trust in Him. He has promised to go before us and prepare the path. He has promised He will never leave or forsake His own.

Dear thirsty one, scan the promises from beginning to end in His eternal Word, remembering they are ordered in all things and sure—each bearing the signature of the Almighty. They touch every phase of our lives, and they are our wealth and our security for they are Yea and Amen in Christ (see 2 Corinthians 1:20). Every promise of His is built on these four eternally solid pillars:

- His holiness means He cannot ever deceive;

- His goodness and grace keep Him from ever forgetting His children's needs;

- His truth assures that He never changes; and

- His matchless power makes Him ever able to accomplish.

O friend, our very thirst, our need (this outreaching of our heart for God) is proof that our need will be met. We need no further proof than our very yearning! God will not mock the hope He gives. Our good Father will surely show His seeking children how to live—really live. "For the Lamb . . . will be their Shepherd, and He will guide them to the springs of the waters of Life" (Revelation 7:17).

Chapter 3

One Desire Only

I *have observed that when I am considering simultaneously the pursuit of eight or ten different desires or goals, it is challenging to decide which one to act on first (with the degree of required determination and effort to carry the desire through to fruition).* My irresolution can tend to precipitate within me a debilitating mental inertia. As a result, while I languish in indecision, my life may come to resemble a stagnant pool (perhaps precariously like those that breed disease). However, I have discovered that when I can direct all my desires into one channel, the result may be more like a river of water that can run swiftly in its allotted course (and can also be accurately aimed to beneficially irrigate the thirsty fields). A highly-focused desire can be like an arrow that goes straight to the target of accomplished purpose.

Many of us have seen how some people seem to be like the notorious flirt—flitting around from one shallow "love" interest to another, obsessed with a score of fancied attractions. In contrast, we pleasurably contemplate the solid satisfaction of people in a relationship stemming from a supreme affection. The difference is obvious. And so we can be blessed when all our desires converge into the single priority of becoming a lover of God, a truly settled friend of the Lord. It is then we can discover the infinitely fulfilling sense of stability and loving intimacy that rewards those who dwell in the secret place of the Most High, abiding under the gracious shadow of the Almighty (see Psalm 91:1).

Just a few short days before the end of Jesus's life on this earth, a certain group of Greeks came to Philip, one of His disciples, with a very specific request: "Sir, we would see Jesus" (John 12:21 KJV). All their desires had powerfully merged into that one intent purpose. It can be a very blessed thing for a man to bring his desires into focus—so they all center firmly on one object. "Blessed *are* the pure in heart, For they shall see God" (Matthew 5:8 NKJV). One aspect of this purity of heart is singleness-of-eye. We become no longer occupied with numerous competing interests apart from God. God Himself has become the exclusive object of our attention. Our hearts echo the apostle Paul's earnest focus of all his aims and purposes into one burning desire—"This one thing I do"—as he spoke of counting all other goals as worthless in comparison with seeking the excellency of the knowledge of Jesus and of pursuing the high calling of God in Christ (see Philippians 3:8–10, 13–14).

The psalmist wrote, "There are many who say, 'Who will show us *any* good?'" (Psalm 4:6 NKJV). All of us have sensed an echo of this cry in our hearts: "Won't someone help me learn how to find that elusive fulfillment, contentment, inner serenity . . . ?" Many people seek satisfaction in earthly comforts, riches, power or fame, pleasure—or in myriad other pursuits. But there is a certain state-of-being that inevitably will rivet all of one's desires away from the general options offered—and instead quite markedly toward a single, very specific preference.

When I recognized my true condition before a holy God (when my heart was awakened by a conviction of guilt for how my egocentricity and rebellion had offended Him, who held my life in His hands) and I perceived my great need for mercy, I had only one desire. Only one. There is only one able Mediator at that specific point of need. Nothing else will satisfy. Like the Greeks long ago, that day I cried out, "Oh, that I knew where to find Him! I must see Jesus!"

All the gold and glitter the world offers could have been poured at my feet then, and it would have drawn no attention from me—for my single cogent desire was, "I must find HIM!" Nor could mere religious doctrines or empty ceremonies and rituals suffice for the burning thirst of my sin-weary soul. My heart cry was "Don't offer me an empty pitcher. Give me water or I die! My only desire is Christ." For there was only one thing that could set me free from the chains of both the guilt of my sin and the power of sin within me. There was only One Person who could make it right between me and my heavenly Father (whom this prodigal had so immeasurably grieved). I yearned passionately and wholeheartedly for mercy, for grace!

When we come to that place—where every power of our being is unified and concentrated into one keenly focused central desire and we would give up everything we ever hoped for in life if we could only have Jesus—then we are very close to coming out of the suffocating darkness and into the daylight. He loves us, and He will respond to such a profound plea and give us our heart's desire. We will indeed see Jesus.

Door of Hope

The desert is where we chose to live. Strange? To some people it may seem so. And yet in the high desert of central New Mexico where we built our home, we found a loveliness in the great brooding stillness. With the foothills of a mountain range close behind us, we can gaze out in the other three directions for miles and miles to other mountains and mesas far in the distance. To us, the big sky and vast expanses of land seem so full of God. We do not wonder that He used to take His people out into such a wilderness to teach them.

There are no man-made distractions here at our desert abode. The deep, winding canyons; the varied cacti and the waving grasses; the long, gently swelling ridges; and the vibrant sunsets painted all across the western sky like a magnificent signature on the end of each day—all are the handiwork of God. Here one's thoughts cannot help but turn to the high places of human thought and ponderings. Come here, and you too will hear the call of eternity in your heart.

There is great value in stillness. In the daily rush of our busy lives it is often challenging to be able to get stilled within. Inner calm eludes us. Even if we can retreat briefly—perhaps into a garden, or to walk along a seashore, or into the privacy of our own chambers—we may yet find it difficult to get still enough to shut out the clamor of the many voices of men and the demanding cries of the cares of life. Something deep within us yearns to feel the pulse of the Infinite, to go away somehow far from life's babbling discords and become attuned to what will connect us with lasting meaning.

There is One who long ago, after looking upon the hard labors of His friends and seeing them weary, even oppressed, said tenderly to them, "Come aside by yourselves to a deserted place and rest a while" (Mark 6:31 NKJV). He still calls to us today, "Come walk with me, come to the shadows of my desert rest, come and just be with me, my child—and I will give you rest. My presence will breathe peace into your restless, weary breast. Only come . . ."

Although our actual desert place has been conducive for us to "come aside" and has greatly facilitated our being able to become stilled within (such that we have found valued rest for our souls), we recognize that going to a specific geographical location on our globe is not really what is necessary. For some that is impossible to do. But there is a way available for every one of us to "come aside and rest a while."

We named our little homestead, our retreat in the desert, the "Door of Hope." No matter how you may have felt in the past about solitude, friend, begin now to try to embrace it. Get alone. Spend time—often and long—alone. Deep within your own heart, it is possible to find your own door of hope.

Chapter 5

Deep Calls to Deep

It is not outwardly, but inwardly, that man will find again the ancient source of his being. Just as commercial fishermen know that fish are to be found in deep water, so it is with us. Our greatest human needs will be met only in the deep things of God. The more we are willing to leave behind the shore and launch out into the deep, the sooner we will discover those realities for which we were born—and for which we were created in His image.

The wise King Solomon (a searcher) wrote this regarding our Maker: "He has put eternity in their hearts" (Ecclesiastes 3:11 NKJV). Innate within our minds is a divinely implanted sense of a purpose, of a profound, enigmatic meaning for our existence. And as Solomon decisively concluded, nothing under the sun (in this world) can satisfy our intrinsic yearning to comprehend that purpose. It is God alone who can. The great depths of our Creator Himself fitted us for the deep—and instilled within us the longing for that depth. Jesus Himself bids us, "Launch out into the deep" (Luke 5:4 NKJV).

We must be still in order to know. "Let be *and* be still, and know—recognize and understand—that I am God" (Psalm 46:10). Although there are many things mankind can learn, do, and accomplish amid the noise and din and chatter of modern life, one thing we cannot hope to learn among the sounds and commotion of the pressing, nervous rat-race of so-called civilization is how to hear the still, small voice of God (see 1 Kings 19:11–12). If we try to reinvent the nature of religious experience, to accommodate it to the blustering and ever-changing surface of things, we will commit a moral blunder of colossal proportions. We seriously shortchange the sincere heart that is groping after God if we offer him a shallow substitute.

There are many false teachers out and about today who purport that as the times change, God's absolutes should change with them. They shout, or cajole, or purr: *Adapt your teachings to the demands of the people! Make them feel as "at home" in the church as they do in the godless world. Certainly don't make them feel uncomfortable by insinuating any embarrassing concept like guilt! If they want entertainment, or if they want their "ears tickled" (with a pleasing philosophy that agrees with their own self-will), or if they prefer compromise with the father of lies instead of following the ways taught by the One who said, "I am the Truth"—well, then just give them what they want!* The grave danger of the reasoning behind this "adaptation" is that although the external conditions of life do change, the soul of man does not fundamentally change.

Beneath the bedlam of the many varied surface phenomena around us, the most basic needs of every human being are all the same. We all are born into sin—that is, everyone of us inherited the rebellious sin nature from Adam and Eve. As such, we stand with our original parents in the same place as they did: outside the Garden, estranged from our Maker. In the final analysis, we are frightened fugitives from the terror of the broken law—of the guilt of our rebellion against our Creator. My greatest need, and yours, is somehow to be rid of my sin, and thereby to be brought again into communion with God. Only then will I be able to obtain the eternal life for which He created me (in place of the tragedy of separation from my Source of true life, a severance which becomes eternal grief).

The essential and vital facts have not changed. Man is still what he has always been. And he cannot save himself from his dire predicament before his holy, offended Creator. When the frenzied extravaganza of civilization's "dance macabre" has ended, judgment is imminent. Man needs a Savior from that deserved judgment. And, thankfully, the Son of Man is forever who and what He has always been—even "from the foundation of the world" (Revelation 13:8 NKJV). And it is He Himself who calls to the eternal in us.

No, the shallows can never truly satisfy us. Our mere natural minds and earthbound imaginations can offer us only flimsy, unconvincing excuses and empty counterfeits. However, the experience with our God that we long for cannot take place on the changing surface of things, but only in the deep, inward part of man—within his human spirit. It is there we are separated from God, and because of this, the very foundation of our life is off-kilter. At our core, things are out of order.

There in that far-down place within us, in primeval silence, our spirit is waiting for freedom—desperate for that quickening word from the Giver of Life that can give it a second birth (the rebirth of our spirits).

Every person (whatever his circumstances, wherever he lives, whatever his experience has been) is made in the image of God. Augustine wrote, "Thou hast made us for Thyself, and our heart is restless until it find its rest in Thee."[3] A voice is calling to every restless soul. It is not like the voices heard throughout the shouting, anxious world. If we will get quiet enough, we will hear the reassuring call of the One of whom it was said, "He shall not strive, nor cry; neither shall any man hear his voice in the streets" (Matthew 12:19 KJV). No, that Voice cannot be heard in the clamor of life's hustle and bustle. But it can be heard in the heart—where it really matters.

The very night before His death, Jesus compassionately turned to His distraught disciples and bestowed on them as a last legacy His own peace. "Peace I leave with you, My peace I give to you" (John 14:27 NKJV). Even though Christ's life outwardly was full of trouble with waves breaking over it like a constant tempest, at any moment people could go to Him and find a great calm, a deep rest within Him. His inner life was like a sea of glass. Far beneath the ocean's surface that may be agitated by driving storms and winds, there is a part of the sea that remains unperturbed. Scientists have called this "the cushion of the sea." The peace Jesus desires to give to us is like that. Below any external adversity, upheaval, difficulty, or distress,

---

3   Augustine of Hippo, *The Confessions of St. Augustine*. (Image Books, 1960).

there lies—far too deep to be disturbed or even stirred—the eternal calm of the peace of God.

The deep within His heart calls to the deep within our hearts, wooing us to come away to the secret place where earth's voices will grow faint and His voice will grow clear. Our heart is yearning for rest. Even in the most hallowed places of earth, we will not fully find it, for the rest we seek is the repose of a heart set deep in God, reconnected to Him. Even now, can you hear the gentle whisper of His call to you, "Come?"

In the Shadow
of a Great Rock

In a desert burning hot, even the sand and pebbles beneath my feet are like coals of fire. The rays of the sun strike like swords. Nothing but an occasional darting lizard indicates to my scorched soul any life can endure here. I feel I am at the end of the earth. How did I get to this place of such aching barrenness?

It may not be a literal desert where you find yourself, friend, and perhaps not exactly the ends of the earth—and yet it feels as though you are at the end of yourself. Within the gloom wrapped around your heart, you feel as though all hope has been incinerated in a furnace. You are so weary you cannot take another step. You feel faint—and ready to die in this lonely place.

For the weak and overwhelmed traveler in a searing desert wilderness, there is a certain sight that will give him hope of survival. Can you see that rock? Yonder in the distance, rising high above the shimmering sands, it stands. It casts a deep black shadow, much higher than the traveler's stature. Long ago, David cried in the wilderness, "From the end of the earth I will cry to You, When my heart is overwhelmed; Lead me to the rock that is higher than I" (Psalm 61:2 NKJV). Fellow traveler, although faint, make for that great rock, and beneath its gracious shade, your spirit will be revived.

Jesus is that great Rock. When you are at the end of yourself, He will bring you to Himself—as the desperately needed shadow from the heat (see Isaiah 25:4). He can be this to you because this Son of Man is higher than you are. He is higher because of His divine origin; higher also because of His perfect obedience; higher too because of His supreme, matchless sufferings on our behalf; and higher because of His overcoming death—and victorious ascent to the right hand of His Father. Dear heart, this Jesus will hide you in the cleft of the rock—His own scarred side.

Chapter 7

In Search of the Fatherland

The place where a person is born is known as his fatherland. No matter where he may live later in his life—either by choice, or by exile, or due to pressing, adverse circumstances—that home country usually retains a deeply meaningful place in his heart. The term *fatherland* evokes emotions related to family ties since it refers to the nation of one's "fathers" (forefathers or ancestors).

Abraham was called by God to go out into a place he was promised would later be his inheritance. Abraham obeyed, not knowing where he was to go. He lived in the land of promise (as did his son, Isaac, and later his grandson Jacob—both heirs with him of the same promise) in a tent, like a mere visitor. During their lifetimes they did not actually receive the land they were promised. It is written they died in faith however, persuaded of the certainty that somehow—some way, some day—they would surely receive from God all He had promised.

We learn from the writer of the book of Hebrews there was something else going on at another level in the lives of these three men (called "the patriarchs" because God promised that their descendants would be a great nation, a nation with a unique calling). Yes, an actual, specific, geographical portion of land on earth would indeed be theirs—as servants of God with a special and holy assignment. But simultaneously, they were looking for "another country." At the same time that they were convinced of a promised earthly possession, in their spirits they "saw afar off" a heavenly country that they also desired.

This vision was not for these patriarchs alone. Countless others who lived before us, a great cloud of witnesses (see Hebrews 11:39–40; 12:1), also caught a glimpse of that better country. All these people walked out their lifetimes on earth as pilgrims—as sojourners just passing through, as it were. They all agreed and acknowledged that this earth was not their true home. They had a homeland, and in the deepest recesses of their beings, they longed for it.

It is written that Abraham was looking for a city of strong foundations whose architect and builder was God Himself (see Hebrews 11:10). It was different from any city built by man, and somehow Abraham (and others of like faith in God) was able to perceive it in the distance. And his inner man welcomed and embraced it. Just as he could have gone back to the wealthy, earthly land of Ur that he had left, he also could have returned to "the good things" this world offered. But Abraham did not want to go back. In their spirits, all who shared Abraham's faith had a different perspective. They were living for heaven—yearning for the things of God. And because that was what they were looking for, and longing for, God was not ashamed to be called their God. He had indeed prepared a heavenly city for them (see Hebrews 11:16).

Abraham lived by faith. He believed in things promised (and hoped for, and patiently waited for his heavenly home). All of us who are Christ-followers are like Abraham: foreigners and strangers on this earth. We are like sheep longing for the fold—and for our Shepherd. God calls us to live by faith (to believe He will fulfill His promises) and to know that our "homesickness" is not for a mere mirage. By faith we press forward, responding to the homing instinct within us, knowing that God will lead and guide us, and trusting fully that He will never leave or abandon us. By faith we strike out for our heavenly home—for the place of His presence.

It may be that the innate recognition of that "city" as our homeland is present somewhere in the hidden depths of our consciousness because it is, in reality, our true fatherland. Perhaps, in a sense, we were once there. Maybe we do not quite wholly feel at rest and at home on this earth because our real home is in the very heart of God, our Father—and always has been.

We Shall Be
Like Him

A sublime and wondrous day is coming on our planet, a day for which creation itself is waiting—even groaning and travailing as if in the pains of labor. Undoubtedly, all creation was affected by man's fall (by Adam and Eve's fateful, rebellious choice to reject the authority of their Creator and to prefer to live independently of Him). Cut off from God, who was their source of life, mankind—and all creation, all of nature—now would experience death. However, it is the earnest expectation of all created things to someday be freed from the workings of death, from the bondage to decay and corruption, to futility (see Romans 8: 20–22). What is it that will happen at that time when even the natural, physical world will be released from the shadow of the curse that sin has brought and will be restored to its original state of perfection? According to Scripture, the whole creation is looking for "the manifestation of the sons of God" (Romans 8:19 KJV)—that is, when they shall be clearly seen by all humanity and known for who they are as God's sons.

Who are the sons of God? The apostle Paul clearly defines them: "For as many as are led by the Spirit of God, they are the sons of God" (Romans 8:14 KJV). And Jesus Himself said, "Whosoever shall do the will of my Father which is in heaven, the same is my brother, and sister, and mother" (Matthew 12:50 KJV). Those who do His will, who are obedient to Him, are His family. Doing God's will (in its most essential and primary form) is simply believing in His Son, whom He sent from heaven to die in our place (see John 6:28–29). Those who have by their belief in Him been thereby justified (acquitted, put back into right standing with God through their faith and trust in what Jesus Christ accomplished on their behalf by His atoning death on the cross) become born again (born from above). That is, these believers experience a second birth in which their spirits (the eternal part of them) are quickened to life. Thus, their spirits will never have to die the "second death" (which, after the death of our bodies, our physical death, is the death of our spirits—the eternal separation of our spirits from God). The promised new heart and new spirit are given to them (see Ezekiel 36:26). They receive the spirit of adoption (of sonship), and their newly liberated spirits cry out with joy to their Father as they are restored to intimacy with Him—and are even made free to call Him "Abba" (Hebrew for "Daddy"). It is then God's own Spirit bears witness in their spirits with deep assurance that they are now indeed the children of God (see Romans 8:15–16).

We are children of God: brothers and sisters of Jesus, now having the same Father. "Go to my brethren, and say unto them, I ascend unto my Father, and your Father; and to my

God, and your God" (John 20:17 KJV). The Son of God came from heaven to earth so we might go from earth to heaven. He took on a body of flesh and blood like ours—to become one of us, fully a man. He became the Son of Man so we might become sons of God. When as the Son of Man, Jesus, rose from the dead, He became the firstborn among men from the dead (see Colossians 1:18). It is written that these brethren of His who would follow Him into eternal life were foreknown (and loved beforehand by God) and foreordained to be conformed to the image of His Son (molded to share inwardly His likeness). They were chosen to be made like Jesus—the firstborn among many brethren (see Romans 8:29). How would we human beings be thus made like Him, like our elder brother?

The writer of Hebrews said Jesus would not be ashamed to call us His brethren because He would sanctify us (purify us, make us holy—even as He is holy). For our High Priest (He who offered and dedicated His very self to become one with us and to suffer death in our place) became our Sanctifier (see Hebrews 2:11). Thus, He Himself would do the work of transforming us, His brethren, through the working of His Holy Spirit and through our belief in, adherence to and reliance on the truth so we "may . . . share in the glory of our Lord Jesus Christ, the Messiah" (see 2 Thessalonians 2:13–14).

"Even as [in His love] He chose us—actually picked us out for Himself as His own—in Christ before the foundation of the world; that we should be holy (consecrated and set apart for Him) and blameless in His sight" (Ephesians 1:4). Long, long ago (before time existed), it was our Father's kind intention and loving plan for us to be adopted as His own children through Jesus Christ so we might be "to the praise of the glory of His grace, by which He made us accepted in the Beloved" (Ephesians 1: 6 NKJV). The awesome fact that God is able to make rebellious, fallen human beings into His own dear children (made again as they were originally created to be, in His image) would bring glory and honor to our Redeemer, Jesus Christ. Our mighty and merciful Savior would be able to victoriously say, "I am glorified in them" (John17:10 NKJV).

Having become the children of God, we are actually made partakers of the divine nature and are thereby able to escape the corruption (decay unto death) in the world. Many, many exceedingly great and precious promises are given to us by God through which we are enabled to progressively partake of our Father's own holy nature (see 2 Peter 1:4). As we choose to yield to His Spirit's leading, we are given grace to be able to, step by step, build character like Christ's (see 2 Peter 1:5–8). Jesus said He did not pray that we, His own, be taken out of the world, but that we be kept from the evil in it (see John 17:15). Here on earth, sin still reigns, and every day we must fight against it in our own lives. But, thankfully, Jesus is within us by his Spirit, and He Himself strengthens us as we challenge the adverse forces that strive to push us from the goal of developing our inner life to align with His. The work begun in us (by our being forgiven and washed by the blood of Jesus, our sinless Redeemer) will surely be completed (see Philippians 1:6). He is even now moving us toward heaven, where there is no more sin and no more curse.

Since we are told we will surely have tribulation as long as we are in this world (see John 16:33), we can expect on our pilgrimage homeward that we will experience trials, struggles, and discouragement. After all, this earth is not our home— Jesus said we are not of this world, just as He was not (see John 17:16). "Here we have no continuing city" (Hebrews 13:14 KJV). While on this earth, our Lord and Master was "despised and rejected of men; a man of sorrows, and acquainted with grief" (Isaiah 53:3 KJV). The beloved disciple wrote, "As He is, so are we in this world" (1 John 4:17 NKJV). How then will you and I choose to view and to deal with the suffering and trials of life on our earthly journey?

In the book of Ruth in God's Word, we read that when her husband died, Ruth chose to leave her homeland and go with her widowed mother-in-law on a difficult journey of unknown outcome. Ruth could have gone back to the ease and comfort of a familiar life in Moab. However, there was no knowledge there of how to find a relationship with the one true God. Ruth willingly gave up everything she knew in order to follow after God with all her heart. To her, no earthly balm or treasure compared with knowing Him. And, in due time, her heavenly Father richly rewarded her hunger for Him and her sacrifice. As children of God, we are His heirs and joint-heirs with Christ, sharing the inheritance of our elder Brother. But it is written that in order to share His glory, we must also be willing to share His suffering (see Romans 8:17). The apostle Paul viewed "the fellowship of His sufferings" as an integral part of the excellence of knowing Jesus and being made conformable to Him. And Paul's heart reached exultantly forward to lay hold of every aspect of that—for which he believed Christ Jesus had laid hold onto him as His own (see Philippians 3:10–12).

To the reality of suffering being part of our lot as God's children, the apostle Paul seemed to convey, "What of it?" He believed the suffering of this present life could not even begin to parallel the blessedness that in due season would be conferred on us as His children! "For I reckon that the sufferings of this present time are not worthy to be compared with the glory which shall be revealed in us" (Romans 8:18 KJV). The appearance of a lowly caterpillar offers no clue or hint of the beauty and exuberantly happy freedom in store for him in the life of a butterfly. After being wrapped in the seeming death of a chrysalis, however, the glorious difference between the beginning and the end will be discovered. "For our light, momentary affliction (this slight distress of the passing hour) is ever more and more abundantly preparing *and* producing *and* achieving for us an everlasting weight of glory—beyond all measure, excessively surpassing all comparisons and all calculations, a vast and transcendent glory and blessedness never to cease!" (2 Corinthians 4:17).

Even though for a while we may be in heaviness and distressed by trials, Peter wrote that the suffering would serve the good purpose of testing and proving the genuineness of our faith in the same way the purity of gold is tried by fire. Responding in faith and trust when we experience painful or troubling circumstances in our lives can produce Christlikeness in us— something very precious to our Father God. Peter continued to explain that although we may be tried for a season, we nevertheless will be guarded and garrisoned by God's power (as we keep the faith) until we inherit completely the fullness of our salvation and adoption—"ready to be revealed for you in the last time—to your honor and praise" (1 Peter 1:5–7, author's paraphrase). The apostle also exhorted us not to think of any fiery trial that might happen to us as a strange thing but instead to rejoice in being a partaker of Christ's sufferings—for if we are reproached for bearing His name, that can even now in this life serve to bring glory to Him (see 1 Peter 4:12–14). A rough diamond being cut on the lapidary's wheel seems to lose much that is of value to it, and yet it is the very cutting process that brings out its greatest worth. We can trustingly submit our souls to our faithful Creator because He knows precisely what He is doing! He is making us into precious jewels that in due time will reflect His own matchlessly glorious beauty (see Malachi 3:17).

Paul encouraged the believers in ancient Corinth to keep on beholding and contemplating the very face of God, as it were, in His Word for we will become like that on which we lovingly fix our gaze—on which we focus our heart's devotion and affection. "And all of us, as with unveiled face, [because we] continued to behold [in the Word of God] as in a mirror the glory of the Lord, are constantly being transfigured into His *very own* image in ever increasing splendor *and* from one degree of glory to another; [for this comes] from the Lord [Who is] the Spirit" (2 Corinthians 3:18). Men become like their ideals—for good or for bad. If we make the Lord Jesus our ideal and trust Him with all our heart, we shall be transfigured—His beauty shall dawn upon our countenance.

The gospel of Christ (the good news of the transforming power of what He accomplished on the cross for us) removed the veil of our ignorance and set our hearts at liberty to run the way of His commandments by faith (that is, by faith in the working of His Spirit in us—doing in and through us what we could never do in our own strength). As we increasingly yield to being led by the Holy Spirit of our Redeemer, we will hear Jesus encouraging us: *Follow Me, and I will make you what you could not make yourself. I will make you channels of My mercy and of My power. I will make you trusting, godly, loving—I will make you like Me.* "'Not by might nor by power, but by My Spirit,' Says the LORD of hosts" (Zechariah 4:6 NKJV).

Although the rest of humanity and all awaiting creation cannot yet see the glory (His own resplendent holiness) God bestows on us who are even now His sons, it shall most assuredly be disclosed one day what we shall be. "Beloved, we are [even here and] now God's children; it is not yet disclosed (made clear) what we will be [hereafter], but we know that when He comes *and* is manifested we shall [as God's children] resemble *and* be like Him, because we shall see Him just as He [really] is" (1 John 3:2). And as we rest in this holy hope, since our Savior is pure (chaste, undefiled, and guiltless), we seek to likewise be pure (see 1 John 3: 3). Our grateful hearts will long to honor Him who loved us and gave Himself for us (who bought us with His own blood in order to glorify us—to raise us to a heavenly dignity). Yes, we would press on toward the goal to win the supreme and heavenly prize to which God in Christ is calling us upward: to know Him and be made like Him (see Philippians 3:12). "As for me, I will continue beholding Your face in righteousness—rightness, justice and right standing with You; I shall be fully satisfied, when I awake [to find myself] beholding Your form [and having sweet communion with You]" (Psalm 17:15*).*

Although as followers of Christ Jesus we may experience hard fare as strangers in a strange land (and be unrecognized and despised now—as our Lord was before us), we do well to walk by faith and to live by hope. Assuredly we can hope and wait patiently with earnest desire for when the Lord Jesus is revealed all at once to everyone on earth, the sons of God will also be revealed with Him (see Luke 21:27; Romans 8:18). Having been transformed into the same image by our oneness with Him, we will be made known as like Jesus, the Son of God!

We are given in the record of Scripture a preview, a transitory glimpse, into the glory of the future manifestation of the sons of God. It is through the experience of the first follower of Jesus who was martyred for his faith: Stephen, a good man and wise, "full of faith and the Holy Spirit" (Acts 6:5 NKJV). As heavy stones broke his body, with his very dying breath, Stephen prayed with love and forgiveness for his murderers— exactly as his Savior had prayed in the throes of agony on the cross for those crucifying Him (see Acts 7:60; Luke 23:34). Even before death as Christ's servant had ushered Stephen into the kingdom of God, this lover of the Lamb was beholding the King in His beauty (see Isaiah 33:17; Acts 7:55–56). And it is written those accusing and attacking Stephen saw his "face [had the appearance of] the face of an angel" (Acts 6:15). His bloody, bruised, and battered face already reflected the glowing light of one transformed into heavenly glory. For a brief moment, Stephen was revealed as a beautiful, beloved son of God!

The fleeting glance of one onlooker in particular (Saul of Tarsus—later called Paul) at that holy radiance on Stephen's countenance profoundly and eternally affected that spectator (see Acts 22:20). He had seen a person made like Jesus (and he had also heard Stephen's echo of the prayer of Jesus). Who knows how that momentary peek at the manifestation of a son of God may have prepared Saul for the magnificent revelation to him soon afterward of the very incarnate Son of God—an epiphany that left Saul mightily changed forever?

Exchanging Weakness for Strength

I *once saw a thought-provoking painting of a heavy rowboat plowing through turbulent waves on a dark and stormy sea.* A broad-shouldered seaman was at the oars, but he was not rowing alone. His young daughter sat close beside him, her small hands also on the heavy oars. Had she been alone trying to manage that boat, what might have been her fate? But a strong man was with her, and her frail efforts were reinforced by his.

It is written of Israel's son Joseph (who had been sold by his jealous brothers into slavery in Egypt) that although the archers shot at him—bitterly attacked and sorely harassed and injured him—his bow remained strong and steady. How is it, we may ask, that this grievously persecuted young man held steady? We can read the unmistakable answer: the arms of his hands were supported and made strong by the hands of the mighty God of Jacob (see Genesis 49:22–24). The image comes to my mind of God's own hands laid over Joseph's hands and arms. I picture my husband's arms around our young son as he ran beside his little bicycle—the father's hands on the handlebars over his son's, holding him safely up as he helped him learn to master the challenge. And this loving, supportive, human fathering is as a mere shadow of our Father God's tender, attentive care for us.

The Lord spoke with clarion promise through the prophet Isaiah: "But those who wait on the LORD Shall renew their strength" (Isaiah 40:31 NKJV). The phrase renew their strength is translated literally as "shall exchange strength." I interpret this as meaning that I can bring my worn-out strength (now depleted, all drained out, leaving only weakness) to my God— and I can exchange it for His strength.

Could this reflect what Paul meant when he wrote, "When I am weak, then I am strong" (2 Corinthians 12:10 NKJV)? He had asked the Lord to remove from his life a very painful, trying thorn in the flesh, but apparently the Lord chose not to. Instead, He instructed His servant (and fortified him) with these words: "My grace is sufficient for you, for My strength is made perfect in weakness" (2 Corinthians 12:9 NKJV). As Paul received and accepted his Lord's will in the matter of the thorn—and grew spiritually through God's guidance— he responded, "Therefore I will rather glory (or boast) in my weaknesses (versus being discontent)—so that the power of Christ may rest on me so that I may be a demonstration, in my weakness, of the strength and power of the living Christ" (2 Corinthians 12:10, author's paraphrase).

Many things are, of course, impossible for man. But nothing is impossible for our God. Thus, when the spirit of a man is in fellowship with the Lord of hosts, the word *impossible* can become itself impossible for him! A deeply concerned and anguished father cried out to Jesus for help for his son who was torn, oppressed, and tormented by an evil spirit: "Can You do anything?" In great compassion, Jesus said to the distraught man, "All things are possible to him who believes" (Mark 9:23 NKJV). Whether our omniscient and all-wise Father delivers us from our suffering, or chooses not to, His will is lovingly purposed to make us strong. And the highest and best kind of strength is being strong in believing Him—in trusting Him. Frederick Faber said, "Ill that He blesses is my good, and unblest good is ill; and all is right that seems most wrong, if it be His sweet will."[4]

Both Joseph and Paul learned to believe in (and trustingly rest in) the Strength that will never fail us. We are not alone in our weakness. Jesus promised, "I will not leave you orphans— comfortless, desolate, bereaved, forlorn, helpless—I will come [back] to you" (John 14:18). Almighty God covers us with His own strength, with His own hands. It is our gracious Father's delight to bestow on His children His perfect strength in exchange for our weakness. We need only bring our weakness (and our hardships, troubles, distress, and failures) to Him, and we will assuredly see the weakness in us transformed into the glory of Christ's own strength. Additionally, we will be His witnesses to other struggling and seeking hearts that His mighty power can do anything! "Is anything too hard for the Lord?" (Genesis 18:14 NKJV).

---

4   Frederick Faber, *The Christian's Daily Challenge* (Harvey Christian Publishers, 1954) 339.

Would We Shutter the Windows of our Souls?

Trying to walk down a wilderness path in the night's darkness is quite different from walking it with a lamp in our hand.

God Himself is our light—and as we live in daily, hourly communion with Him, it is in that very proportion that we are enabled to walk in the light (in ways of safety). Our steps will be treading the crystal pathway of light if we are living in a manner such that His name and nature are ever precious to our hearts. The name of Jesus will be always relied on for strength when temptation is near and will also be frequently linked with praise on our lips. Walking in His light will mean as well that we will be transparent before Him. We will not hide any secret sin—rather we will habitually seek cleansing from anything that would separate us from our Father (who is pure and holy). "But if we walk in the light as He is in the light, we have fellowship with one another, and the blood of Jesus Christ His Son cleanses us from all sin" (1 John 1:7 NKJV).

Walking in the light also implies being obedient to his revealed will—led by Him as our Master. That is, in order to remain in His light, we will submit to His lordship and obey His precepts, acknowledging that "the commandment of the Lord *is* pure, enlightening the eyes" (Psalm 19:8 NKJV). It is written that it is in God's light we are able to see: "With thee is the fountain of life: in thy light shall we see light" (Psalm 36:9 KJV). Thus, walking as children of light (that is, in fellowship with Him who said, "I am the light of the world"), our understanding becomes increasingly enlightened and our minds purified.

In contrast, when we are alienated from our Father, our understanding becomes darkened, and we are not able to perceive the truths of God. In this state, we are very vulnerable to being deceived by counterfeit "lights." Dangerously, when we continually choose to incline our hearts toward rebellion against God's ways and toward wickedness, we will eventually give up our souls to darkness. Making a trade of cleanness for uncleanness, we soon will be walking in the mere emptiness and futility of our own blinded minds (see Ephesians 4:17–19). Then it will be as if the light of the glory of God in the face of His Son Jesus beats against a shuttered window in vain. If our heart becomes hard toward our Creator (and we then refuse to glorify Him as God and are unwilling to be thankful to Him), then disastrously we shut out from our soul the vitalizing light of God (see Romans 1:21).

Since God is our very source of life, when we spurn His light, locking it out of our souls, we also foolishly and tragically reject His life for us! Speaking of the incarnate Word of God (God's own Son, Jesus Christ), the apostle John wrote, "In Him was Life, and the Life was the Light of men. His life is the light that shines through the darkness, and the darkness comprehends it not—(but) the darkness can never suppress or overcome it" (John 1:4–5, author's paraphrase). Would we be so grievously reckless as to devastatingly shutter the windows of our souls against God's light—and life?

Selling All to Buy the Field

Jesus described the kingdom of God as being like something very precious and valuable hidden in a field—that if a man should find it, he would be joyfully willing to sell all he had so he could buy that field to obtain the treasure (see Matthew 13:44).

Some of us have a deep hunger inside us—a hunger for the Truth. We may have sought down avenue after avenue that claimed to lead to answers but found none of them satisfied us. We discovered sadly that all of them, after all, were empty promises. Like the stories of the Old West when a man tried mine after mine to find silver or gold, we may have explored one so-called "truth" after another—always coming up empty-handed. Our efforts were frustratingly futile. The Truth we longed for evaded us. And, woefully, we found ourselves on the precipice of despair.

There is a man who claimed to be the Son of God and said, "I am the Truth" (see John 14:6). If our yearning is an honest one, and it is the Truth that is genuine knowledge of God that we indeed seek, the Scriptures tell us He will be found by us—if our seeking is earnestly wholehearted. "Then you will seek Me, inquire for *and* require Me [as a vital necessity) and find Me; when you search for Me with all your heart" (Jeremiah 29:13).

He comes to the heart that is hungry in order to fill it. His Spirit is very willing to show us the path to the treasure for which we yearn. He is faithful to teach us that the starting point on that path is the fear of the Lord—that is, that worshipful reverence for His holiness and taking God seriously—is the beginning of wisdom and understanding (see Proverbs 9:10). Only as we originate our quest at that wellspring alone will we be guided to the fountain of life (see Proverbs 14:27).

But consider well, fellow searcher: the person who earnestly and seriously seeks diamonds, or precious pearls, or gold will focus his entire undivided attention on his pursuit. He will be willing even to leave his native land, if necessary—willing, indeed, to leave everything that other men hold dear. And this is how it must be for us if we are to truly find the knowledge of God. We must be willing to lose anything, even perhaps everything (willing to "sell all we have") in order to buy the field with its incomparably priceless hidden treasure.

For the Truth, There Is Always a Price to Pay

Lies are cheap. They are freely available and abundant anywhere and everywhere in our world. But for the Truth, there is always a price to pay.

If we are not willing to pay the price of our own humbling, we cannot buy the Truth. The most valuable earthly things are procured at high prices. And the sore cost of bruising (that leaves us broken in our self-will) produces great, incomparable value in us in God's sight. Humility is part of the price for Truth, for it is the humble and meek who can receive the guidance of God's light.

Patience is another currency we must use to buy the Truth. To those who are willing to wait on God (and for God) with steadfast endurance, divine light is given. The fact that He is the source of all Truth compels us to submit to His sovereignty and timing. If we impatiently insist on quick verdicts and demand our own conclusions, we will not find the Truth.

It is the hottest fires that refine gold. And our faith in God (which is much more precious than gold) is likewise purified and proven in the burning crucible of life's adversity. In the fire, however, we shall not be burned (see Isaiah 43:1–2)—only that which binds us will be. Similarly, purity of soul costs us the Refiner's fire—as does the acquisition of any eternally precious thing. It is the pure-of-heart whose eyes will be enlightened to see the Truth.

Fourth (and ultimately), the price of obedience is all important and indispensable if we would buy the Truth. We cannot truly know God's will and His ways (which are the nucleus and essence of Truth) if we are not prepared to unquestioningly and unrestrainedly obey the Truth of His will that He would show us. Wholehearted obedience is required to buy the Truth—and to keep it.

We can deceive ourselves if we presume that we have the Truth when all we really have is a cheap, easy, counterfeit "truth" for which we paid no price. At the end of all things, any spurious substitute for the Truth will disastrously fail us—becoming to us the fatal tragedy of tragedies. However great the cost may be to us, surely it is wisdom to sincerely and earnestly want our lives and faith to be founded on the eternal Truth of God.

Like a String
in a Cave

Many of our difficulties and sorrows in life have come to us because we have chosen our own path, done our own will, rather than seeking God's will for our lives. Long ago the wise leader Moses exhorted the Israelites to stand still and "hear what the Lord will command concerning you" (Numbers 9:8 NKJV). Hearing His commands and obeying that voice when He speaks in our hearts is the secret to a blessed life.

The path of obedience will sometimes take us through the dark. Although for awhile the path may seem mysterious and obscured, it is nevertheless the way. When Noah began walking with God, he certainly did not know all that lay ahead. The bare word of God that he obeyed collided with common sense and natural experience. In obeying it, he was at odds with all that was familiar in life—even with the entire human race. And yet, without any precedent, he still chose to walk one day at a time in obedience to God's command, for he trusted his Almighty God. Day by day his trust grew stronger and stronger as he held on to God's word tenaciously. Noah undoubtedly grasped it as intensely as miners seeking exit from the deep dark of underground tunnels keep their hand firmly on a tiny cord until they reach the first streak of light.

Many times in obeying God's directions, we also must learn the art of waiting. Noah's true heart did not fail him, although he had to wait a hundred and twenty years to see the fulfillment of God's word to him. There is often great strain in waiting. Rather than bearing it, the natural man may choose an easier way—perhaps rushing into the fray in desperation, taking the alternate course of doing something to "help" God. But to toil on faithfully as Noah did, without results, in quiet obedience— that is hard indeed. It might even completely wear down our fragile hope unless our hope is firmly anchored beyond life's ebb and flow.

They Shall Hunger No More

They shall hunger no more, neither thirst any more . . . For the Lamb which is in the midst of the throne shall feed them, and shall lead them unto living fountains of waters: and God shall wipe away all tears from their eyes.
Revelation 7:16–17 KJV

When my father died, these verses took on precious meaning to me. They spoke to my heart with a great assurance that gave me deep joy. The days of my beloved father's hunger were over. Beyond the consideration of merely natural, physical hunger, I was comforted for him regarding certain other hungers he felt during his earthly life—the fulfillment of which seemed to evade my dear father this side of heaven.

It is God Himself who gave us our bodies—the amazing instruments through which our soul and spirit can realize His life plan for us. And having placed these wonderful machines into our custody so we could accomplish all He assigned us to do, surely He correspondingly pledged Himself to provide for our physical life (for the maintenance of its needs and strength). As the writer of Proverbs said, He will "feed me with the food allotted to me" (Proverbs 30:8 NKJV). The Amplified translation renders this "the food that is needful for me," implying that in God's granaries full of wheat and other needed nutriment, there is my needed share—already calculated for and provided. Jesus taught us to pray asking for our daily bread, and surely we can trust in His faithfulness to answer that prayer.

But there are other things we human beings hunger for, and there is other "food" that is needful. There are hungers other than that of the body. Our Creator is fully aware of these hungers in us, for indeed, they are God-given desires. And as surely as He provides for our bodies, He also wants to meet these needs of ours—hungers of the heart and of the mind. We all hunger for the daily bread of love and of acceptance and belonging. We hunger for meaning and significance. Our inner beings also yearn to be satisfied somehow, someday, as we hunger and thirst for righteousness. We need the daily bread of high thought and purpose. We have deep cravings, too, for hope. Since it is God who gave us these needs, He Himself likewise takes the responsibility for meeting the needs.

For these types of hungers in particular, however, we human beings are liable to fall into the error of trying to meet them by taking things into our own hands. We may be tempted to gratify our desire for love apart from God and His ways. We are often apt to seek knowledge in ways not illuminated by the light of eternal Truth. We choose our own way, rather than our Maker's. We tend to act at the dictates of passion and unwisely take our lives out of God's hands. If we will instead dare to trust

Him, we will inevitably discover our gracious, loving Father will supply without fail all our needs. Those who throw all the responsibility on Him will not and cannot be disappointed in their faith.

Most of all, we were created with a built-in hunger for God Himself. We hunger for fellowship spirit-to-Spirit with our Creator. Jesus said, "I am the bread of life. He who comes to Me shall never hunger, and he who believes in Me shall never thirst" (John 6:35 NKJV). With unwavering certainty, we may say of those who have learned to be satisfied with God, "They shall hunger no more." The prodigal son at long last realized of his good father that even his father's hired servants had enough to spare. Oh, child of the great Father, there is plenty for you! As we seek first of all His kingdom (His rulership over our lives) and aim at and strive after His righteousness (His way of doing and being right—and right-standing with Him through His appointed way: His Son, Jesus), we can be assured and confident all else we hunger for and need shall be given to us (see Matthew 6:33).

SECTION II

Starting Off

The Highest and Best Knowledge

You or I may know a great deal about someone famous— innumerable facts about such things as his family, his childhood and personal history, major occurrences in his life, many of his actions as well as his thinking and decisions, and his character and values in general. If, however, you were to walk up to the door of his house or his office—say, for example, the Oval Office—simply declaring, "I know him!" and expect a hearty welcome, you most likely would not be admitted anywhere near this person you "know" so well. Obviously, there is a vast difference between knowing about someone and actually knowing that person. It is possible to have many opinions about God, but it is quite another thing to truly know God.

Being really acquainted with someone implies a two-way relationship, one of depth and mutuality. Although we may not realize it, the greatest human need is a relationship with God. More than ever, it seems stress is the catch-all disease of the age in which we live. But the basic human need is the same as it has been for countless centuries ever since Adam and Eve were expelled from the Garden of Eden. We are weary from trying to live life without God. We were made for a relationship with our Creator—made to know our God. The knowledge of God and Christ capable of transforming our lives into what they were originally intended to be when God created us is more than intellectual perception or assent to a creed. Truly knowing God is an experience of Him (through a deep spiritual union with Him)—made available to believers through the incarnate Son of God, Jesus Christ.

The only accurate basis for this genuine knowledge of God our Maker is the Scriptures (the Word of God). Even so, knowing the Word is not enough. Jesus reproved the Pharisees for searching the Scriptures and yet refusing to come to Him—about whom the Scriptures testified (see John 5:39-40). What the Bible says about God is there to lead us to a personal relationship of intimate love with Him. It teaches us that God rewards those who diligently seek to know Him (see Hebrews 11:6). And amazingly, He desires to reward us with the greatest gift He can give us—Himself. He told Abraham, "I am your exceeding great reward" (Genesis 15:1, author's paraphrase). May we not settle for any lesser gifts from our good God than the Giver Himself!

Two of the greatest twentieth-century Christian writers wrote striking statements that, although contrasting, if taken together offer a quite balanced perspective of foundational importance. C. S. Lewis believed **the most important thing about a man is how God sees him** (that is, what God thinks about man—what our value is to Him).[5] It is clear throughout the Bible that God places tremendous significance on man, the only being created in His image and the very center of His love and affection. Also, men (not angels or any other beings) are the object of His redemptive work—and given the potential of becoming His sons. From God's point of view, if you or I were to have a price tag put on our lives signifying our value to Him, we are worth the blood of His Son, Jesus Christ. We could not be more valuable! Do we deeply know that this is our Father's heart toward us?

On the other hand, A. W. Tozer wrote, "**The most important thing about a man is what he thinks of God**"[6] (that is, how a man thinks about God—how he perceives God). If what we think about God is inaccurate and does not reflect His true character and nature, we will not be able to come into a genuine relationship with Him. Catherine Marshall wrote this:

I have come to believe that only if we can depend upon the Creator as a God of love shall we have the courage and confidence to turn our life and affairs over to Him. What builds trust like that in the Creator? Only knowing Him well—His motives, His complete goodwill—and being certain that no pressures will make Him change.[7]

Similarly, just as I cannot convey to someone the sweetness of honey unless I have tasted it myself, without the reality of

---

5   C. S. Lewis, *The Weight of Glory* (William B. Eerdmans Publishers, 1985).

6   A. W. Tozer, *The Knowledge of the Holy* (Harper and Rowe Publishers, 1961), 9.

7   Catherine Marshall, *Moments That Matter* (Thomas Nelson, 2001) 204.

a true acquaintance with God on my own part, how can I tell another spiritually hungry person how sweet and satisfying that experience is? I myself must be fully persuaded by personal experience of the singular wonder of the one true God. "Who is like You, O Lord, among the gods? Who is like You, glorious in holiness, awesome in splendor, doing wonders?" (Exodus 15:11).

At one point in His ministry, Jesus asked His disciples who people were saying He was. They answered that some thought perhaps John the Baptist, or Elijah, or one of the old prophets who had come back to life. Then Jesus pointedly asked them, "But who do you [yourselves] say that I am? And Peter replied, The Christ of God!" (Luke 9:20). And, indeed, this is the essential question each one of us human beings must inevitably resolve. Who do you say Jesus is? If we know little of the excellencies of Jesus (and what He has so graciously done for us—and is doing now), we cannot love Him much. But the more we truly know Him, the more we will love Him—for to know Him is to love Him. When my heart becomes deeply convinced of His overwhelming love for me, it is then that genuine love for God is born in me. At our conversion, God's Spirit bears witness with our spirit that we are His children (see Romans 8:16). That is when truly knowing—and loving—our Father can begin.

The answer for all life's stress, for all mankind's needs, can be distilled down into one single, small step. It is to respond to an over two-thousand-year-old invitation (that is as fresh and viable today as it was then): "Come to Me, all you who labor and are heavy-laden *and* over burdened, and I will cause you to rest—I will ease *and* relieve *and* refresh your souls. Take My yoke upon you, and learn of Me; for I am gentle (meek) *and* humble (lowly) in heart, and you will find rest—relief, ease and refreshment and recreation and blessed quiet—for your souls. For My yoke is wholesome (useful, good)—not harsh, hard, sharp or pressing, but comfortable, gracious and pleasant; and My burden is light *and* easy to be borne" (Matthew 11:28–30). Come to Jesus. And in coming to Him, there will come to you the knowing of Him—the best and highest knowledge.

When We Know
Our Source

When a man knows his source, he can begin to be what he was intended to be. Jesus said, "He who has seen Me has seen the Father" (John 14:9 NKJV). It is in seeing Jesus that we see our Maker, our Source.

We have many unanswered questions. In so many ways we are bound up—like the woman bent over for many long years who could do nothing to lift herself up. We feel our hope is like a bird with a broken wing—and our poor, weary hearts are discouraged. But long ago the gracious Master walked into the synagogue where that woman was and spoke authoritatively, "Woman, you are loosed from your infirmity," and immediately she was "made straight" (see Luke 13:10–13 NKJV). The same Jesus will walk today into our lives, into our homes, into our situations of need—if we will give Him a chance. His touch still has its ancient power to heal the brokenhearted, to give sight to the blind, and to set the captives free (see Isaiah 61:1–3; Luke 4:18). For that is just what He came to this earth to do—

and He is living still and is able and willing. No one can remain broken or crooked or crippled if he grips the hand of the Lord of Life.

Even the best the world can offer us cannot provide the satisfaction our hearts need. Only God can slake our thirst and satisfy our longing. Our problem is that we do not know God. "Thus says the Lord, Let not the wise *and* skillful person glory *and* boast in his wisdom *and* skill; let not the mighty *and* powerful person glory and boast in his strength *and* power; let not the person who is rich [in physical gratification and earthly wealth] glory *and* boast in his [temporal satisfactions and earthly] riches; But let him who glories glory in this, that he understands and knows Me (personally and practically, directly discerning and recognizing My character), that I am the Lord Who practices loving-kindness, judgment and righteousness in the earth; for in these things I delight, says the Lord" (Jeremiah 9:23–24).

He is very willing to make Himself known to us, but there are conditions. No part of our nature must be barred off from God, nothing at all in our hearts hidden away behind a curtain—but every room within our beings and our lives must be trustingly open to Him. Above all, there must be surrender. All that we are and have must be His. If we will get on our face before Him, He is ready to reveal Himself to the sincerely seeking heart. And when we know Him (and are known by Him), we will be made whole—we will become what we were meant to be. And we will be at rest.

How Does God Define Eternal Life?

Jesus was praying to His Father very near the end of His life on earth when He spoke these words: "And this is eternal life, that they may know You, the only true God, and Jesus Christ whom You have sent" (John 17:3 NKJV). God defines eternal life in terms of the substance of our relationship with Him. Continuing to pray to His Father, Jesus said, "I have manifested Your name—I have revealed Your very Self, Your real Self—to the people whom You have given Me out of the world" (John 17:6). According to Jesus, perceiving and recognizing who the Father and His Son really are (being truly acquainted with Him and understanding Him) is what constitutes eternal life. Life eternal, then, is not mere conscious and unending existence but a life of acquaintance with God in Christ.

God spoke through the prophet Jeremiah that a day would come for Israel when "they all shall know Me, from the least of them to the greatest of them" (Jeremiah 31:34 NKJV). When

God brought Israel out of Egypt, He made a covenant with them to be as a husband to them. But they broke that covenant, and their hearts turned away from a loyal relationship with God. Centuries later, God promised to make a new covenant with them, and this one would be different—His Law would not be something external to them but would be within them, written on their very hearts. This New Covenant would bring them back into relationship with Him: "I will be their God, and they shall be My people" (see Hebrews 8:10–11 NKJV). This turning away from our Maker (resulting in our separation from Him)—and this opportunity made possible for us to truly turn again to Him and be received—is a picture in miniature, as it were, of all humanity.

Our rebellion against the sovereign Creator (who both made us and loves us) produced a rift—a huge chasm—between Him and us. "Your iniquities have separated between you and your God, and your sins have hid His face from you" (Isaiah 59:2 KJV). How could we possibly make peace with an offended God? How could we come home to our Father? The blood of bulls and goats (or even as some dared attempt, the sacrifice of their own children) could not take away sins (see Hebrews 10:4; Micah 6:7). There was only one way for guilty mankind to be reconciled to God. "Then [God] is gracious to him, and says, Deliver him from going down into the pit [of destruction]; I have found a ransom [a price of redemption, an atonement]!" (Job 33:24). God has reconciled us to Himself by the death of His Son Jesus Christ: "God was in Christ reconciling the world to Himself, not imputing their trespasses to them . . . For He made Him who knew no sin *to be* sin for us, that we might become the righteousness of God in Him" (2 Corinthians 5:19, 21 NKJV). The sum and essence of the Christian religion (and that which distinguishes it from all other religions) is the atoning sacrifice of God's own Son, Jesus Christ, to pay for our sins—to ransom us from eternal death by paying the penalty for our sins. This holy, incalculable sacrifice made Him our great Mediator with the Father. And in this the love of God for us is manifested (see 1 John 4:9–10).

Men have sought to obtain eternal life through many schemes of idolatry and philosophy and other human-based and human-initiated plans. Many gods are worshipped, but the Christian worships only One—the living and true God. (Although the Jew, the Deist, and the Muslim profess to acknowledge one God, they do so without acknowledging the need for any atoning sacrifice or mediator.) The true Christian approaches God through the great Mediator, whom we believe is equal with the Father. The Son of God qualifies as our Mediator between us and God through His having, for our sakes, become incarnate (that is, by taking on a flesh and blood body like ours), so He could experience death—in order to die as our substitute that He might thereby reconcile us to God. "For it pleased *the Father that* in Him all the fullness should dwell, and by Him to reconcile all things to Himself, by Him, whether things on earth or things in heaven, having made peace through the blood of His cross" (Colossians 1:19–20 NKJV).

To be reconciled means to "make peace with." When two people argue, if they desire to be reconciled and reach an agreement, one must yield, giving way to the other. This is what God did for us; He Himself restrained His wrath and waived His rights. We rebels could not ever provide what would be required to make peace with God. Therefore, through the offering up of His own Son, God made peace with us! It is written of Jesus, "He Himself is our peace" (Ephesians 2:14 NKJV). A peacemaker who tries to separate two people fighting will often receive more blows than those wrangling. Christ mediated an agreement between God and us, and it cost Him the pain and suffering of the cross. How is it now that we can appropriate this reconciliation, this peace with God? "Acquaint now yourself with Him [agree with God and show yourself to be conformed to His will] and be at peace; by that [you shall prosper and great] good shall come to you" (Job 22:21).

Thus Jesus, God's own Son—whom the Father's love gave to us as a propitiation for our sin (see 1 John 2:2 NKJV)—is the Mediator of the new covenant: "When supper was ended, He took the cup also, saying, This cup is the new covenant [ratified and established] in My blood" (1 Corinthians 11:25). "This is my blood of the new testament, which is shed for many for the remission of sins" (Matthew 26:28 KJV). While Jesus was on the earth, He glorified His Father—He made known to us the Father's nature. The glory of His Father was always His goal. The completion of His work of making God known as who He really is was the joy set before Him—for which He endured the cross and despised the shame (see Hebrews 12:2). This glory, this knowledge of Himself, was the goal and the end of the sorrow (travail) of His soul, and in obtaining it, He was fully satisfied (see Isaiah 53:11). And through the Son's willing offering of Himself to His Father's will, Jesus Christ was glorified and honored by His Father— Jesus Himself being made the bridge for us back to our Father's heart (see John 12:28; 17:5). Eternal life could not be given to believers unless Christ, their Surety, both glorified the Father and was glorified by the Father (see John 17:1–2). This glory (this making known of the Father and of Christ, whom the Father sent) is the sinner's way to eternal life.

What does it mean to "know" the Father? It is much more than just apprehending facts about Him. It is having the right view of Him. And that will include all the impressions on one's mind and life that an accurate perspective of Him will produce, such as a "fear of the Lord" (a worshipful reverence and deep respect); gratitude; a sincere desire (birthed out of our love toward Him in response to His first loving us) to obey Him, yielding our wills to His will; honor of His holiness by nurturing purity and holiness in our lives; and supreme affection. It means, of course, knowing Him as He is (as He reveals Himself to us—not as we merely imagine Him to be). Jesus clearly specified in His definition of eternal life that knowing God embodies recognizing Him as the only true God. This means we acknowledge Him as the only cause and end of all things (in contrast to all false gods). In all forms of sinful idolatry, honor due to God is turned aside from Him and bestowed, instead, on that which is not God (either on some of His creatures or on some manmade invention or assumption). Knowing God in truth means we perceive and appreciate Him as the One to whom alone belongs the reality of the idea of God (see 1 Corinthians 8:4).

The way for us to obtain eternal life also entails knowing "Jesus Christ whom You have sent" (John 17:3 NKJV). God sent His Son into the world to declare His own attributes and character.

It is only in Jesus, the Messiah, the Word made flesh, that we can clearly hear God's voice of mercy, forgiveness, love, and fatherhood. "And the Word was made flesh, and dwelt among us, (and we beheld His glory, the glory as of the only begotten of the Father,) full of grace and truth" (John 1:14 KJV). The very juxtaposition here of knowing both God and Jesus Christ (as stated in this identification of what is necessary for eternal life) unmistakably implies the godhead of Jesus. It is inconceivable that the knowledge of God and the knowledge of a creature could equate to eternal life. "In the beginning [before all time] was the Word [Christ], and the Word was with God, and the Word was God Himself" (John 1:1).

When the Creator God made the first man, Adam, he was but dust until God breathed the breath of life into him (see Genesis 2:7). That original life was eternal life—for man's spirit was intended to live forever. This "forever life" was through fellowship with our Maker (the Source of life). Adam's rebellion against God (the very fountainhead of his life) broke off that communion, which itself constituted the eternal life of his spirit. As the oak tree is within the acorn, all of us human beings were in our father, Adam—and thus the whole of mankind lost in Eden the very essence of life for which we were created. Since separation from God is death, every one of us sons and daughters of Adam needs deliverance from the fate of death.

The word *sent* in the definition of eternal life that Jesus gave is highly significant. It is in the sending of His Son that God provides that which alone can save us—which can make us anew a "living soul." Thus, it can be extrapolated that the Father cannot be known except in and by the Son. "Therefore if any person is (ingrafted) in Christ, the Messiah, he is (a new creature altogether,) a new creation; the old (previous moral and spiritual condition) has passed away. Behold, the fresh *and* new has come!" (2 Corinthians 5:17). Thus, Jesus Christ's coming to earth was necessary for the restoration of the knowledge of God (and thereby eternal life) to Adam's lost race.

To know Jesus Christ, whom He sent is much more than being aware of information about Him or having a mere concept of Jesus as in any ordinary notions of men. To know Him is to have a correct and just view of Him in all His perfections as both God and man—as a mediator, prophet, priest, and king. Knowing Him does not begin, of course, until we see that we are sinners and recognize and feel our need of such a Savior. We begin to truly know Him only when we receive Him, as we yield our whole souls to Him—trusting His love for us. "And we [have seen and] know [positively] that the Son of God has [actually] come to this world and has given us understanding *and* insight progressively to perceive (recognize) *and* come to know better *and* more clearly Him Who is true; and we are in Him Who is true, in His Son Jesus Christ, the Messiah. This is the true God and Life eternal" (1 John 5:20). Knowing that He is a Savior perfectly suited to our needs (and that it is only in His hands that our souls are safe), we will then allow His character and His work to make their due impression on our hearts and lives. We will choose to believe in Him—and, trusting Him, to love and obey Him.

The life Jesus lived (and the life He gave as the atonement for our sins, which had separated us from our God) consisted in and was maintained by His own knowledge of the Father. It was by making known to men this God (and thus glorifying the Father) that Christ gave men eternal life. This indeed is our Father's heart toward us: "He who did not spare His own Son, but delivered Him up for us all" (Romans 8:32 NKJV). The sending of Jesus was thus necessary to this knowledge of God's loving intent for us—and necessary so we could receive the free gift of salvation (deliverance from death, the wages of sin). Jesus, as our ransom (by becoming a curse so we would not have to be accursed), bought back for us what we had lost in Eden. He bought back for us eternal life through restored fellowship with our Maker. "Now all things *are* of God, who has reconciled us to Himself through Jesus Christ" (2 Corinthians 5:18 NKJV). This is the vital principle of the Christian religion.

The focus of the new covenant is a people who know their God—and allow Him to live through them. The night before His death on the cruel cross, Jesus explained to His disciples that the imminent sacrifice of His life would mean for them possession of eternal life. He said He would raise up at the last day those who "eat My flesh, and drink My blood" (meaning those who dwell in Him, and in whom He dwells as their very life—just as He Himself lived through vital fellowship with His Father): "Whoever eats My flesh and drinks My blood has eternal life, and I will raise him up at the last day. For My flesh is food indeed, and My blood is drink indeed. He who eats My flesh and drinks My blood abides in Me, and I in him. As the living Father sent Me, and I live because of the Father, so he who feeds on Me will live because of Me. This is the bread which came down from heaven—not as your fathers ate the manna, and are dead. He who eats this bread will live forever"

(John 6:54–58 NKJV). By this we are taught how to have an interest in Christ—through whom eternal life is God's gracious and undeserved gift.

There is rescue from death (that is, everlasting separation from God as judgment for our sin) as our eternal destiny only through repentance (changing our minds about sin) and trusting in what Jesus's death on the cross and His resurrection achieved on our behalf. "There is salvation in *and* through no one else, for there is no other name under heaven given among men by *and* in which we must be saved" (Acts 4:12). True assurance, protection, and security are provided and available through dependence on God (my decided choice to depend on His designated provision for me to be able to return to a relationship with Him).

For God so greatly loved *and* dearly prized the world that He [even] gave up His only-begotten (unique) Son, so that whoever believes in (trusts in, cleaves to, relies on) Him shall not perish—come to destruction, be lost—but have eternal (everlasting) life. For God did not send the Son into the world in order to judge—to reject, to condemn, to pass sentence on—the world; but that the world might find salvation *and* be made safe *and* sound through Him. John 3:16–17

Since the final judgment of our lives and what infinity holds for us will be determined by whether we have come to know the Lord (according to His own terms—not ours—for knowing Him), it is unmistakably indispensable to grasp that our lives are essentially defined by whether we have a desire to know

Him—to know Him in truth. The apostle Paul expressed his own emphatic choice compellingly:

[For my determined purpose is] that I may know Him—that I may progressively become more deeply and intimately acquainted with Him, perceiving and recognizing and understanding [the wonders of His Person] more strongly and more clearly. And that I may in that same way come to know the power outflowing from His resurrection [which it exerts over believers]; and that I may so share His sufferings as to be continually transformed [in spirit into His likeness even] to His death. Philippians 3:10

The high calling for every human being is to know God—and, secondarily, to make Him known.

Made for Something

We hardly notice sparrows. The death of a single sparrow would likely be too trifling for us to note. Yet Jesus said God takes account of even seemingly so insignificant an occurrence as a sparrow's falling to the ground (see Matthew 10:29). Not one sparrow can perish without the knowledge and consent of a loving Father. The Creator of the whole universe has a will regarding even one sparrow. God Himself is a participating presence, a God who is there—even in this tiny event in His world.

Jesus went on instructing His twelve disciples through this analogy: "You are of more value than many sparrows" (Matthew 10:31 NKJV). If our Creator knows (and cares about) every sparrow to such a degree, how much more must He know and profoundly care about us? Every one of us is infinitely precious in our Father's sight, and He knows every single detail about us—even to the number of hairs on our head (see Matthew 10: 30). Jesus told His followers therefore to fear not. Nothing can happen to us without His knowledge and His consent—

and His participating presence as our Savior. He has a will for each sparrow, and He has a will (a specific plan and purpose) for me—and for you.

God is a God of purpose. Creation was no chance accident—but was the expression of a definite purpose in His heart. And our divine Maker unquestionably has made us for something. He has made us according to the good pleasure and kind intent of His will (see Ephesians 1:5). Since He has made us for something, would it not seem to be essential for us to find out what His purpose is—so we can wholeheartedly aim toward its accomplishment?

I once walked through a museum full of exhibitions of machinery. I would stop at one and wonder, *What is this for?* I'd muse over another, *What could that be for?* I was sure the maker of the machine intended for it to accomplish something specific—for why make a machine that is not meant to accomplish something? Indeed, we can never begin to understand a complicated machine until we know what purpose its designer and maker had for it.

The writer of the letter to the Ephesians continued by describing the "something" that God made us for: "[So that we might be] to the praise *and* the commendation of His glorious grace—favor and mercy—which He so freely bestowed on us in the Beloved" (Ephesians 1:6). The purpose in God's heart for us (from "before the foundation of the world") was that we be adopted by Him—"(consecrated and set apart for Him) . . . in love" (Ephesians 1:4). To make us into His own image (thus able to fellowship as one with Him in a relationship of love) is the object of God's workmanship in creating mankind. May we willingly respond to so loving and good a plan for us—for nothing short of this will accomplish His divine purpose in our creation. Do you doubt that a purpose for your good could be His plan for you—and that He cares specifically about you? Remember His sparrows!

We Existed in His Heart

Consider this: God knew us—perfectly—long before we had any knowledge of Him. "For You did form my inward parts, You did knit me together in my mother's womb. . . . Your eyes saw my unformed substance, and in Your book all the days *of my life* were written, before ever they took shape, when as yet there was none of them" (Psalm 139:13, 16). Yes, before we were birthed into this world, we existed in God's heart!

Joseph's brothers, out of envy and malice, had sold him as a youth into cruel slavery in Egypt. Many years later during a time of famine in their land, they came to beg for food before him (as the second-in-command in Egypt). They did not recognize the very changed Joseph—but Joseph certainly recognized them. And despite all the deep suffering they had caused him, Joseph yet loved them (see Genesis 42:8). When the brothers discovered who this mighty potentate (who held their very lives in his hands) actually was, they justifiably feared him. But they didn't need to, after all.

Even when we had made ourselves His enemies, the Lord our God knew us—and lovingly yearned for us. When we finally left the misery and foolishness of our wicked rebellion and came to God in weeping repentance, at first we may have viewed Him inaccurately—as only an angry judge. In ignorance, we feared and mistrusted Him, and we guarded our hearts from Him, not able to fully believe His words of grace. But Jesus saw us as His beloved brothers—as infinitely the objects of His heart's deep affection. "The Lord knoweth them that are his" (2 Timothy 2:19 KJV). He knows and loves His own just as much when they are prodigals feeding the swine (yet unaware of the true nature of their Father) as when they have at long last opened their hearts to know and trust Him—and have freely given Him their love. And just as Joseph did for his brothers, Jesus graciously invites us to come up and sit at the table with our royal Brother.

Not Good Enough for God to Love Me

Does God love only good people? Do we have to be a certain kind of person for God to love us? Do we have to first get straightened up and attain some evasive high standard of character before He can love us? The answer is an emphatic no!

How can I make such a confident assertion? Because God's own Word, the Bible (which some call God's love letter to us) states this: "God shows *and* clearly proves His [own] love for us by the fact that while we were still sinners Christ, the Messiah, the Anointed One, died for us" (Romans 5:8). You see then— God loves sinners.

It is true that when I become profoundly aware that I am a sinner (one who has rejected His lordship, choosing to be an enemy of God), I indeed may feel unworthy of His love. But His promised love and care are not based on my feelings. "But God, who is rich in mercy, for his great love wherewith he loved us, Even when we were dead in sins, hath quickened us together with Christ, (by grace ye are saved)" (Ephesians 2:4–5

KJV). In other words, even when we were slain (disconnected spiritually from our Source of life) by our own trespasses (rebellion against our Maker) because of His love for us He made us alive—in fellowship and union with Christ.

I can become a child of God when I believe Jesus is the Son of God and that the Father demonstrated His love for us by sending Jesus to become flesh and blood (Immanuel, one of us) and to be the atoning sacrifice for our sins (see 1 John 4:2, 9–10). As I put my faith in Jesus and trust in what He accomplished on the cross (where He died in my place), I am positioned to be able to receive the free gift of a restored relationship with my Maker—the reconciliation which this incomparable act of love made available to me, a guilty sinner. I can receive mercy (forgiveness and pardon that I in no way have earned—rather than the punishment I deserve) and can receive grace (that is, what I don't deserve: unmerited favor, the goodness and blessing of God—His kindness extended to the unworthy). To those of us who will believe, God gives us the very life of Christ Jesus Himself—the same new life with which He quickened Him from the dead (eternal life). I dare not presume to doubt so great a promise (and so magnificent a demonstration) of His love for needy sinners!

It is fear that makes me doubt He could love me. I fear what He as a righteous Judge may do to me. I sense acutely what, as a sinner and rebel against Him, I do indeed deserve (condemnation to death—in the sense of eternal separation from God). Again, let us look to His "love letter." The apostle John wrote, "There is no fear in love; but perfect love casts out fear" (1 John 4:18 NKJV). We need have no fear of someone who loves us perfectly. We who have believed His love (as indisputably manifested in God's gift of His only begotten Son to us—and in the Son's taking upon Himself the punishment we deserved for our sin) no longer need to fear or dread God's holy judgment against us. We who believe do not have to face that terrible judgment that all those who refuse to accept Jesus as their substitute on the cross must certainly face. God's perfect love for us can eliminate all fear, all our dread of punishment from Him—if we will just receive His appointed provision for our sin (that which has separated us from Him). If we still fear Him in the sense of being judged or punished, it is because we do not yet accurately comprehend how much God loves us each individually—or we do not yet really know Him (not perceiving His true character).

Jesus revealed to us one of the most illuminating of all the names mentioned for God in the Bible: Father. God is much more than all that we think of as best in earthly fathers. He is the one, after all, who made fathers—and mothers! God is good—simply good and wholly good—therefore, He must be a good Father. He is a Father who is both willing and able to supply all His children's needs, who is tender in His love and full of compassion toward them, and who will be on their side against the whole universe if necessary. Unrest of spirit and discomforting fear become impossible to souls who come to truly know God as their loving Father.

When Jesus ate with tax collectors and notorious sinners, He was severely criticized for befriending "such people" by some of the people who considered themselves good (and who felt comfortable and secure in their self-righteousness). Jesus's retort countered His accusers: "Those who are strong *and* well have no need of a physician, but those who are weak *and* sick" (Mark 2:17). Would anyone logically expect a doctor to refuse to treat the sick? It would be just as absurd for Jesus to refuse to deal with acknowledged sinners (with those erring ones, those who knew they were not able by their own effort to be free from the bondages of their sin and the destruction it wreaked in their lives). He continued in the same verse, "I came not to call the righteous ones *to repentance*, but sinners." He was well aware that people who think that by their own self-effort and good works they can earn right standing with God are not able to see their own need and "sickness" in God's sight. Jesus likened Himself to a physician who goes where there is genuine and acknowledged need.

The apostle Paul knew very well what great wrongdoing he had been capable of, and he distinctly knew what he was at the core. He saw himself as the chief of sinners (see 1 Timothy 1:15). Yet this same Paul also drank deeply of the height and depth and width and breadth of his Father's love (see Ephesians 3:14–19). No doubt it was with those two realities side by side in his mind (as necessary as both railroad tracks are to balance a train) that he wrote to his young protégé, Timothy, "The saying is sure *and* true and worthy of full *and* universal acceptance, that Christ Jesus, the Messiah, came into the world to save sinners, of whom I am foremost" (1 Timothy 1:15). Through acquaintance with the compassionate heart of Jesus Christ, Paul had come to perceive that God's mercy and grace and tender lovingkindness abound far beyond His righteous judgment toward sinners (see Romans 5:20).

So if you are struggling with the opinion that perhaps you are not good enough for God to love you, may I suggest to you, dear one, that you may be asking the wrong question. Perhaps the better point of view to consider is this: "Will I believe that God loves me—even me?" In faith, take your stand here:

"Therefore, since we are now justified—acquitted, made righteous and brought into right relationship with God—by Christ's blood, how much more [certain is it that] we shall be saved by Him from the indignation *and* wrath of God. For if while we were enemies we were reconciled to God through the death of His Son, it is much more [certain], now that we are reconciled, that we shall be saved [daily delivered from sin's dominion] through His [resurrection life]" (Romans 5:9–10).

No matter how things may appear as doubts assail and bombard you, friend, let your heart cast out its fear! Choose to trust in your Father's great love and in what the Son of God did on the cross to prove that love to you. "He who did not withhold *or* spare [even] His own Son but gave Him up for us all, will He not also with Him freely *and* graciously give us all [other] things?" (Romans 8:32).

Two Messages

All of us yearn to be accepted and to be loved. This is a core need, part of our deepest being.

It doesn't take very long as we walk along our life journey from day one until something happens that results in the opposite experience for us: rejection. And we are wounded. For some of us, the wounds are very, very deep. For all of us, not being accepted in one way or another distorts how we feel about ourselves. We get the message that we are not worth being accepted. And a shadow begins to fall over our lives.

The message of our being acceptable or not acceptable (or of having worth or not having worth) comes to us most often through the vehicle of other people in our lives. The problem is that this avenue of delivering such a significant message is many times not a dependable avenue. We live in a world that makes demands on us to perform to a certain level to be accepted. If you can meet a certain standard, then you are valuable. If you "pass the test," then you are "in." Otherwise, you are "substandard" or a "reject." Other people most typically can offer us only this conditional love. Because we are a fallen race of people living in a fallen, sinful world, our fellow human beings cannot give us an accurate view of our worth.

The most damaging result of our experience with rejection is that we begin to assume God assesses our worth in the same way—conditionally (based on our performance). But that is a very erroneous assumption. Our value to God is in no way conditional. We are not accepted by Him because we prove we are valuable. We are of immeasurable worth to Him simply because we *are*—not because we can do anything or become "good enough." Each of us is loved by God for who we are—created by God our Father as a unique and special individual. His love for us is unconditional! This is the other message—one from a higher source—that can quench our seemingly insatiable inner hunger.

What a risk God took by putting us into a world where fallible human beings so often give us the message of our significance! How confusing, broken, and tragic the messages can be—either because of the inability or because of the sin of the messengers. Even the very best of parents can inadvertently start us down the wrong track of getting a distorted message.

Our natural tendency is to believe the lie that we must gain a sense of worth by something we can do. We work to earn both value and security by our performance—a painfully elusive goal. Even if we feel we can perform adequately to be confirmed and applauded by other people, that acceptance is a poor substitute (even in a sense a counterfeit) of that genuine product for which our hearts yearn. Our true need is for acceptance simply for who we are—because we are— not for what we do. How greatly God desires for each of us to come to know the truth of His unconditional love for us!

Our inner beliefs are the foundation of our lives. Our enemy, Satan, wants to undermine and erode any belief on our part that we could be loved just for who we are. He desires to keep us hopelessly bound in a never-ending struggle to earn acceptance. Of course, our heavenly Father's will for us is that we would want to do what is right and would try our best, but He also wants us to know that whatever the results of our efforts are, we can still be totally accepted and secure in His unchangeable love. When we believe the enemy's lie of conditional acceptance, we come under the power he wields through fear. We are driven to strive to do what others require of us, and we come up with elaborate schemes to protect ourselves from any failures to measure up. Inevitably, however, we all fall short of becoming "good enough." Then feelings of worthlessness feed our sense of rejection. And Satan delights in our bondage.

"You shall know the truth, and the truth shall make you free" (John 8:32 NKJV). The spirit of rejection that has infected the entire human race commenced in the Garden of Eden when man rejected God. That is the root of the disease. What, oh what, then could be the cure? What is God's answer to this problem that evolved from the Fall—the eclipsed knowledge of the possibility of relationships based on unconditional acceptance? Jesus is the answer! Jesus, the Son of God, went to the cross to make a way for man to return to God. The poison of rejection brought to us by mankind's rejection of God was laid upon Jesus at Calvary. And as the great exchange (see

2 Corinthians 5:21) was taking place (as Jesus became our sin so that in Him we could become the righteousness of God), He shouted out that awful cry, "My God, my God, why have You forsaken me?"

How unbearable that cry of all cries must have been to the Father's heart! And yet even before the foundation of the world, both the Father and the Son were willing for that unparalleled estrangement—the "forsaking" that precipitated that agonizing cry. Jesus went through the inconceivable darkness and desolation of separation from His Father so you and I would not have to ever again be separated from Him. Our Savior stood where His believers will never have to stand—and that is the real heart of the atonement.

He bore the sin of our rejection of God (and of our rejection of one another) so that if we believe, His righteousness could be imputed to us. Each one of us now could choose (through being "in Him" and identified with Him) a lifestyle of acceptance. That holy exchange opened for us—for you and for me—the possibility of a life of abundant joy in place of our impoverished, joyless life of rejection. Jesus experienced all the pain of our wounds of rejection so that in coming to Him, we could receive comfort and healing—yes, even release from every trace of rejection the Fall brought. By the death of the Son of God (in our place, for our sin and guilt before God), the door was opened for us to come Home (accepted back into God's heart). The truth that liberates you and me is that we are "accepted in the Beloved" (Ephesians 1:6 NKJV)—as we are in union with God's dearly loved Son.

With which message defining your worth will you agree? We all have a choice.

He Finds Me Lovely

Friend, can you hear deep in your spirit the soft, sweet wooing of the heart of God? He is even now reaching out to you in His tender love—yearning for you to simply come and be with Him a little while. If you get still enough within, you may hear Him gently entreating, "Come, beloved one, sit at My feet. Talk to Me—I love to hear your voice." You may think (as we all do at times), *Surely He could not be pleased with me, and I would not be welcome in His holy presence.* But this is not the heart of our gracious Father!

Yes, it is true that we indeed may have grieved Him with our sinful choices to act against His will (a good and perfect will that is always for our good as His dearly loved children). But consider His grieving: Long ago, the crowds in the day when Jesus was taken to the cross to die, shouted, "Crucify Him" (proclaiming thereby that they refused Him as king). Even so, amid His pain and anguish, remarkably, Jesus prayed and asked His Father to forgive them "for they know not what they do" (Luke 23:34 KJV). Perhaps without even fully realizing what we were doing, our attitude often has been like that of the vinedressers in the parable who first killed the vineyard owner's servants he had sent to them—and then later killed the owner's very son—a veiled picture of how humanity would treat God's own Son (see Matthew 21:33–40). Our hearts too may have rejected Jesus, in essence saying, "We will not have this *man* to reign over us" (Luke 19:14 NKJV). And now, rightly and appropriately, we do feel unlovable. To feel no guilt, no regret for doing wrong, and no accountability to anyone (as some proponents of modern psychology's unrealistic type of self-esteem tout—wanting to make us feel good about ourselves at the expense of truth) is dangerously building our hope on a false premise.

But, dear heart, if honest pangs of conscience have made your soul uneasy, I must try to convey to you that one of the most beautiful words in the human language is *forgiveness*. In contrast, *sin* is a bitterly sad word indeed—for sin has been the cause of all the sorrow, violence, shame, heartache, agony, and tragedy that have burdened mankind since the beginning of time. But the word *forgiveness* is so supremely and exceedingly beautiful—because God's precious forgiveness cancels the effects of sin! Truly, we can greatly rejoice and be everlastingly thankful that "there is forgiveness with thee" (Psalm 130:4 KJV).

Most notably however, our forgiveness is costly—immeasurably costly. Yes, the Father's great love toward us offers forgiveness without cost to us. But it cost God Himself the unfathomably stupendous price of giving up His beloved Son to be the propitiation (payment and appeasement) for our sins (see 1 John 4:10). God offered Jesus as the atoning sacrifice that made reparation for our guilt before Him. "For He made Him who knew no sin *to be* sin for us, that we might become the righteousness of God in Him" (2 Corinthians 5:21 NKJV). This was the great exchange! It made us what we ought to be—and made us acceptable and in right standing again with our Father. Now, friend, see in the dear face of your Father the marvelous light of forgiveness as He looks upon you—and know that He finds you lovely. "To Him Who ever loves us and has once [for all] loosed *and* freed us from our sins by His own blood . . . be the glory and the power *and* the majesty and the dominion throughout the ages *and* forever and ever. Amen" (Revelation 1:5–6). May you and I never cease to worship in wonder at the price Love paid!

So, longing one, hear now the sweet music of the invitation of Jesus: Come! Come freely, without cost—and for your soul-thirst, drink the matchlessly refreshing water of life from the fountain of His love (see Revelation 22:17). For He who gave His very life to provide forgiveness for you finds you entirely loveable—and He delights in you! If you have returned unto the Lord from a long estrangement and have believed and received the treasure offered to you by the great exchange, then you are covered by His mercy, having received His abundant, all-encompassing pardon. Nothing now can separate you from "the love of God which is in Christ Jesus our Lord" (Romans 8:39 NKJV).

And now, will your heart reciprocate so great a love?

In His Hand

The whole round world and all its inhabitants (and much more) lie in the hand of God.

In Psalm 136 (NKJV), the statement "For His mercy *endures forever*" is repeated twenty-six times. Mercy that lasts forever. Mercy for any and all who will receive it from Him is available— forever. Pause and think on that! The psalmist looked back over all mankind's history, from creation through all the time his mind could review (including all his personally stormy and troubled days), and he wrote those words. He repeated and repeated them because throughout all that long span of days his heart perceived a thread—the thread of God's mercy. This mercy (God's loving-kindness, His steadfast, unfailing covenant love) is enduringly offered to every human being.

Brighter even than the sun and moon is this light (the forever mercy and grace of God)—like a silver gleam, shining surely and everlastingly above the murky darkness of this world's strife and chaos. Oh, if only we had eyes to see it always! Deeper than the weight of all my sin (even below this pit into which I have dug myself), the hand of my God upholds me. The love of God is deeper still! "Underneath *are* the everlasting arms" (Deuteronomy 33:27 NKJV). And underneath my falling is His forgiveness—and His mercy that endures forever.

It endures forever! Can I then suppose it could ever fail me? Jesus said of His sheep (those who received Him, to whom He gave eternal life) that they would never perish: "My Father, which gave them me, is greater than all; and no man is able to pluck them out of my Father's hand" (John 10:29 KJV). Nor can I ever just accidentally fall out of the arms of God's mercy. Yes, I can choose to worry and fret like a restless baby. But if I were to just calm and still myself, surely I would see above me (like a mother's sweet face) His faithful love embracing me—His cherished child.

Oh, may I ever trust in that mercy! His great mercy has neither a beginning nor an end. God, whose very nature is love, has always loved, He loves now, and He always will love. That incalculable, endless love is reaching out to me—and to you—this very moment. I pray that you come to believe His eternal word: "I have loved you with an everlasting love" (Jeremiah 31:3 NKJV). May you know, deeply and assuredly, that you are in His hand—cradled in His compassionate, boundless mercy.

Five Times Never

We sometimes may feel that God has forgotten us. We think He has left us to bear our trials on our own. Perhaps at first when we face a difficulty, we rally like good soldiers. We resolve to march out against the distressing situation under the banner of trusting in our God because we have believed His word that He will fight for us. We feel certain that with the right attitude and earnest faith, defeat of our enemy is imminent.

But time passes. And then more time passes. And fight as we may, nothing seems to change. The days wear on, and we grow weary. We begin to lose our nerve, our stamina. We are now threatened even more perhaps than by the trial's severity, by its longevity. Questions pierce our hearts like fiery darts: *Why would God let me suffer so long? Has He forgotten me? Has my seeking to live for Him been in vain, after all?*

We are not the first ones to ask those questions. Long ago the children of Israel were convinced the Lord had forgotten and forsaken them. But the Lord affirmed to them that was something He absolutely could not do! He asked of them a rhetorical question regarding whether a nursing mother could forget her child. Even though very unlikely and against nature, some human mothers might. Yet, in comparison, God said of Himself, "Yet I will not forget you. See, I have inscribed you on the palms *of My hands*; Your walls *are* continually before Me" (Isaiah 49:15–16 NKJV).

During a long trial, it comes easily to us to wonder if we have fought in vain to keep the faith. But here again is assurance: "I said not unto the seed of Jacob, Seek ye Me in vain" (Isaiah 45:19 KJV). In other words, God says He did not call them to a fruitless service. He had certainly not said to them, "Seek Me for nothing" (as if He had told them to ask something of Him that He really did not plan to give)! On the contrary, God went on to emphatically state, "I the Lord speak righteousness— the truth [trustworthy, straight forward correspondence between deeds and words]. I declare the things that are right" (Isaiah 45:19). And again through His prophet, He assures His people, "Remember these things [earnestly] . . . you shall not be forgotten by Me" (Isaiah 44:21).

If we find ourselves in an agonizing place of seeming abandoned and cry out to God in anguished prayer, we can remember there is Someone who knows exactly how we feel. God the Father has heard that cry from his own Son— on the cross. Ponder, then, dearly beloved, afflicted one, this astounding and amazing fact: The Father deliberately turned His back on His own Son so He would never have to turn His back on us. And because of this awesome, holy truth, you and I can patiently endure—for decidedly and surely He will be with us and will keep us and will bring us into the land He has spoken about to us (see Genesis 28:15).

God Himself has indisputably told us, "I will never leave you nor forsake you" (Hebrews 13:5 NKJV). Interestingly, the original Greek uses five negatives and can thus be rendered, "I will not, I will not leave you; I will never, never, never forsake you." The words could not be better arranged to express stronger consolation and confidence. Hold on to this precious promise of the unchangeable goodness and friendship of God toward you (toward all those who put their trust in Him). Although our eyes may not see it now, the one who trusts in Him absolutely, positively will be blessed! He who is the Rock of our strength, the Rock of ages, has steadfastly promised us, "I will not in any way fail you *nor* give you up *nor* leave you without support. [I will] not, [I will] not, [I will] not in any degree leave you helpless, *nor* forsake *nor* let [you] down, [relax My hold on you].—Assuredly not!" (Hebrews 13:5).

Jesus Touched Lepers

*L*eprosy has affected humanity for thousands of years, especially in ancient times when there was a severe social stigma associated with it. Because the debilitating and disfiguring disease was contagious, most cultures required that lepers be separated from other people, and many lived in leper colonies. No one wanted to be exposed to the offensive and dreaded disease. People with leprosy were forcibly shunned as "unclean," so in addition to their physical suffering, they experienced the emotional pain of being ostracized from family and friends—and isolated from the rest of society.

Although people had justifiable fear of the disease of leprosy, Jesus touched lepers. "And behold, a leper came up to Him and prostrating himself, worshipped Him, saying, Lord, if You will, You are able to cleanse me by curing me. And He reached out His hand and touched him, saying, I will; be cleansed by being cured. And instantly his leprosy was cured *and* cleansed" (Matthew 8:2–3). This poor trembling man, deeply distressed and yet daring to be hopeful, fell on his face before this one Man—wondering if He would be different from all others. *Could there be mercy for me, even me? Would He be willing?* Perhaps somewhere within his lonely heart and his mind tortured with sadness, the leper remembered words spoken centuries before by a prophet of God: "A bruised reed He will not break" (Isaiah 42:3 NKJV). And his faith arose to believe in that tender love. This One will not push me aside as I deserve. It is written of Him that He came to heal the sick, to set the captives free, and to bind up the broken-hearted (see Isaiah 61:1; Luke 4:18). And Jesus, moved with compassion, did not disappoint the man's faith in Him!

In those days, leprosy offered no hopeful signs, no token of recovery, and it yielded to no human remedy. However, when the darkness of primeval chaos had heard the voice of the Almighty command, "Let there be light," the darkness had to yield to light. And at the word of the Lord Jesus, Son of the Almighty God, leprosy had to obey Him and flee at once! "I am indeed willing. Be thou clean," He spoke to the kneeling, beseeching leper, "and the leprosy departed from him, and he was cleansed" (Mark 1:40–42, author's paraphrase). This unclean person broke through ceremonial regulations of the law of his time and pressed into Jesus's presence. And Jesus Himself broke the human law to meet the desperate man's need. Jesus casts out no one who comes to Him (see John 6:37).

Let us consider now the grave reality that the effects of sin on a person bring him into a much more miserable state than does leprosy and result in a much more hopeless plight for him. However, the same hand that touched lepers and healed them is also willing to touch sinners and make them clean. The hand that saved sinking Peter will reach out to every sinking sinner who seeks mercy—and in a moment, will both save him from drowning and make him clean.

It is a most gracious work of God's Holy Spirit to convict our hard, blind hearts of sin (and how it separates us from our holy God). When we are blessed by this conviction, then in His loving compassion, He can enlighten our understanding as He gives us the invaluable gift of being able to look on the Son of God pierced by our sins—bruised for our sakes (see Isaiah 53:8). When God's hand is thus mercifully upon us, revealing to us the immensity of the price He paid to reconcile us to Himself (the offering on the cross of His own beloved Son, who willingly took our sin upon Himself), surely we will begin to desire intensely that a clear light search all the corners of our hearts and root out every trace of sinfulness. When we have been brought to clearly see our sin (which at root is rebellion against God's having authority over us) and how we have so greatly offended God our Maker, we will be deeply sorrowful with a holy despair as we begin to comprehend our sin as the greatest evil. Our blind eyes will be opened to the tragic grievousness of sin—to its odiousness for relentlessly and inevitably destroying us and everything good in our lives, as well as for the terrible price it cost God. We then will no longer embrace it as a friend or coddle it like a harmless pet—instead we will spurn it in its dreadful, deadly reality. And we will prize our Savior above all things.

Jesus is the hope of every human being—of all of us. In such immeasurably deep love for us, He "Himself bore our sins in His own body on the tree" (1 Peter 2:24 NKJV). In the garden of Gethsemane when Jesus drank "the cup" His Father had given Him (see Matthew 26:39; John 18:11), He imbibed into His own sinless person all my sin, all yours—yes, all the sin of everyone who has ever lived or ever will live. Jesus Christ, the Son of God, actually became (was endued with) our sin! "For our sake He made Christ [virtually] to be sin Who knew no sin, so that in *and* through Him we might become [endued with, viewed as in and examples of] the righteousness of God" (2 Corinthians 5:21). We could become by His boundless goodness and His inestimable sacrifice what we were born to be and ought to be: in right relationship with Him—acceptable and approved! This is what I call "the great exchange." The contemplation of this exchange must surely bring the most reverent awe to our grateful, humbled hearts—just as do the words of the old hymn "And Can It Be That I Should Gain?"

> And can it be that I should gain
> An interest in the Savior's blood?
> Died He for me, who caused His pain—
> For me, who Him to death pursued?
> Amazing love! How can it be,
> That Thou, my God, shouldst die for me?
> Amazing love! How can it be,
> That Thou, my God, shouldst die for me?[8]

---

8   Words: Charles Wesley, *Psalms and Hymns*, 1738. Music: Thomas Campbell, *Bouquet*, 1825. "And Can It Be That I Should Gain?" *Cyber Hymnal*: http://www.cyberhymnal.org/htm/a/c/acanitbe.htm (April 5, 2018).

Indeed, how can it be that a king would leave his throne and die for his subjects? Who can begin to explore this great mystery that the Creator died for His creatures, that the Immortal died for the mortal? And, yes, the Innocent for the guilty? It is God's matchless, immense mercy, His beautiful, infinite grace—that is it! There can be no question of my Master's affection for me, no doubt ever again—for I can feel the closeness of His embrace, He who has loved me with such a love as this. Notwithstanding all my provocations, rebellions, and resistance to His Holy Spirit's wooing, my long-suffering Savior patiently bore with me. His love never let me go! It is available for every one of us to discover the truth of His words: "I have loved you with an everlasting love" (Jeremiah 31:3 NKJV).

Do you feel, sinner, that you are like a leper, too wretched to come out of hiding - out of a sense of banishment from humanity—perhaps fittingly an outcast? Oh, hear your Redeemer's loving voice calling to you, "If any man is thirsty, let him come to Me and drink!" (John 7:37). He has already provided all any man needs to quench his soul's thirst. Sinfulness of character is no barrier to the invitation to believe in Jesus, to stoop down and take a deep drink of the flowing flood of His forgiveness and love. Come, sinner, to Jesus, believing in his mighty substitutionary work, and you will soon learn the power of His gracious touch. The Lamb of God will lead you to fountains of waters of life—and God will wipe away every tear from your eyes (see Revelation 7:17).

Unclean, blistered, leprous lips may touch this stream of divine love. They cannot pollute it—but will be purified as they drink of this life-giving water Jesus alone can give. Though the sinner's soul be utterly famished, the Savior can and will restore it. Despite our perceived wretchedness, Jesus, full of grace, entreats us, "Come to Me and drink" (John 7:37 NKJV). It is written that Jesus cried those words. Even now, He cries out to us, no doubt with tears—yes, for us who caused Him to shed His blood! Jesus pleads with us to be reconciled to our Father through what He did on our behalf. Believe, friend, that you (yes, even you) can confidently rest your head on the bosom of your Lord Jesus—just as His beloved disciple John rested there, leaning against His heart. Come to Him then, for He longingly waits for you—to be gracious to you, to show His lovingkindness and peace to you (see Isaiah 30:18).

Why Spend Your Wages for What Does Not Satisfy?

We live in this world in which there are "actors" who put on a very convincing show. Nevertheless, in the end it is merely a show, and it will leave a sting when the watchers who thought it was real and permanent realize it was not. Many people look on various scenes of life's drama and conclude they have found what is fully true, substantial, and enduring.

Imagine, for example, the joys of finding one's life partner, marrying, and soon being surrounded in your loving home by your own beloved children. Some people are convinced that the word *home* is as sweet as any so-called heaven. Thus contented, they may say, "Just give us this happiness, and we will be fully gratified. Let those religious fanatics seek dreamy joys that they call eternal—but this is enough for us!" Yet we are all dying creatures. Inevitably the scene will change in one way or another.

Another day will bring another scene—this time perhaps one of sorrow, trouble, or loss. Then conversely, we may be prone to think this is what is more real (as it is so fiercely penetrating and feels as if it will surely last forever). Hear this actor's lines: "I will never again be able to lift my head. Everything worth living for is gone!" But once again the person, now mourning, does not see that the things of earth are not the whole picture. If he rejects faith in God, then he forfeits that which would help him believe there is hope for a heaven beyond earth. Significantly, the sorrows of time are one thing, but immortal sorrows are entirely another. Nor will this person be likely to open his heart to consider that even in the here and now, believers in God as an all wise and loving Father often testify that He has produced lasting good for them through their very trials.

There are countless other scenes. Here is a successful businessman who is confident he has attended to the one real necessity in life. Look there, as he sits back with his arms crossed smugly across his chest, fully convinced he can have a perpetual feast because of his substantial financial assets. He laughs at immortality, at accountability to a Creator, and at faith and mockingly taunts those who speak of a spiritual and supernatural realm as fools. "Waste your time praying and all that if you want to. But I will eat, drink, and be merry for I have accumulated right here on earth plenty of what can make anyone content," he scoffs. He does not recognize if that is all he has, he is actually a very poor man. "How is it that such a man, with his vast and seemingly solid earthly security, could be poor?" you may ask. Because in the most tragic type of madness, he chose to give up his eternal soul to win what he cannot take with him when death inevitably comes to his door. His treasure was only for a brief time. For his eternity, he stored up no treasures—nothing at all like treasure (see Luke 12:16–21).

Ah, people, why be so gullible to be cheated by the world's actors. Why do you so easily believe these acts in life's play are sufficient to fully satisfy and are secure and lasting when in reality they are temporary and as mere shadows? As you gaze, convinced and enraptured, on this stagecraft I present to you, will you listen to a true friend whisper into your ear that indeed there is something else? It is what alone can (and will) profoundly and genuinely satisfy. For fellowman, your deepest desires are of a larger span than what this world can offer—and only the Infinite can fill them.

Wait *and* listen, every one who is thirsty! Come to the waters; and he who has no money, come, buy and eat! Yes, come, buy *priceless* [spiritual] wine and milk without money and without price [simply for the self-surrender that accepts the blessing]. Why do you spend your money for that which is not bread? And your earnings for what does not satisfy? Hearken diligently to Me, and eat what is good, and let your soul delight itself in fatness [the profuseness of spiritual joy]. Incline your ear [submit and consent to the Divine will], and come to Me; hear, and your soul shall revive; and I will make an everlasting covenant *or* league with you, even the sure mercies—kindness, good will and compassion. Isaiah 55:1–3

Call on Him –
and Be Astounded

"*Daddy, help!*" What loving father when he hears such a cry will not run to his child's aid as fast as he can? Or when a mother discerns her grown daughter's sad countenance veils a broken heart, will she hear the girl's unspoken cry and quickly go to her with a listening ear and comfort? These types of human responses are merely echoes of the desire in God the Father's heart to come to the aid of His children when they cry out in need to Him. If a man's son were being cruelly taunted and badgered by a bully at school and the lad bore his painful ordeal in silence out of fear of the bully, when the boy's father later discovers the facts, would he feel grieved that his son had not called on him for help? Do we grieve God when in our determination to be independent (to live life on our own without Him), we perhaps inadvertently scorn our Father's tender entreaty to let Him help us? He is a gentleman of the highest order and as such will not force Himself on us. Yet how many, many times in Scripture is God's loving inclination toward us divulged by His heartfelt plea, "Call on Me"?

"Call to me, and I will answer you, and show you great and mighty things, which you do not know" (Jeremiah 33:3 NKJV). The Lord is telling His people through the prophet when they call upon Him in their distress, He will answer them not only to save them but to do so in ways that will astound them! "Now to Him Who, by (in consequence of) the [action of His] power that is at work within us, is able to [carry out His purpose and] do superabundantly, far over *and* above all that we [dare] ask or think—infinitely beyond our highest prayers, desires, thoughts, hopes, or dreams— To Him be glory" (Ephesians 3:20–21). This is our Father's heart—so full of above-and-beyond grace toward us!

At the time God spoke this message through Jeremiah to the people of Israel, they were full of guilt before Him because of their iniquity and rebellion against Him. Indeed, they had brought upon themselves the chastening that captivity in Babylon would mean. Yet their Father God implored them to turn around and again call upon Him, for even though their immediate future was one of desolation, that was not His will for their final destiny. Although He is a God of truth and of justice, He is also a God of great compassion—and "plenteous in mercy" (Psalm 86:15 KJV). In any trouble or distress, His gracious message to us remains, "Call upon me—and I will deliver you!"

There are stipulations, however, regarding the nature of our calling on God for help. God will not be mocked (see Galatians 6:7). He is not a puppet that any man can control. It is written of Jesus that He knows what is in man (see John 2:24–25). God searches the heart and knows all our thoughts (see Psalm 139:1–3). If we want Him to hear our cry and draw near to us in our distress, we must call on Him in sincerity. "The Lord is near to all who call upon Him, to all who call upon Him sincerely *and* in truth. He will fulfill the desires of those who reverently *and* worshipfully fear Him, He also will hear their cry, and will save them" (Psalm 145:18–19).

An essential ingredient in this necessary sincerity is the willingness to turn from our wicked ways of rejecting His will and to forsake the paths that have lead us into our trouble. Where there is a heart contrite and broken for its sin, God is very nearby—and that is the time to seek Him, for although our thoughts may indeed condemn us, we may discover that His thoughts toward us are quite otherwise.

"Seek, inquire for *and* require the Lord while He may be found—claiming Him by necessity and by right; call upon Him while He is near. Let the wicked forsake his way, and the unrighteous man his thoughts; and let him return to the Lord, and He will have love, pity *and* mercy for him; and to our God, for He will multiply to him His abundant pardon. For My thoughts are not your thoughts, neither are your ways My ways, says the Lord. For as the heavens are higher than the earth, so are My ways higher than your ways, and My thoughts than your thoughts." (Isaiah 55:6–9).

Oh, may we be truly thankful to this God who so loves us and who is so graciously ready to hear us when we repentantly call upon Him! "For You, O Lord, are good, and ready to forgive [our trespasses]—sending them away, letting them go completely and for ever; and You are abundant in mercy *and* lovingkindness to all those who call upon You" (Psalm 86:5). This is indeed amazing grace!

God promised the people through Jeremiah that if they would call upon His name (recognize and acknowledge His nature), He would not only answer them and come to their aid in their difficulties and suffering but would also reveal to them "great and mighty things" (see Jeremiah 33:3). The Hebrew word used here for *mighty* means "inaccessible, isolated" and conveys the sense of things hidden and fenced in. The Lord was telling His people that if they sincerely called on Him, He would give them revelational insight into things that could not otherwise be known. The Father's heart desired to reveal to His children things that on their own they could not distinguish and recognize or have knowledge of or understand. These revelations are described as "great"—and would, without a doubt, remarkably bless and benefit those who called upon Him. What amazing and astonishing provision this promise entails!

The apostle Paul wrote to the followers of Jesus in Rome of the reality that so often we "do not know what we should pray for as we ought" (Romans 8:26 NKJV). We may not know what prayer to offer or how to offer it worthily. Of course, we long to pray effectively, and we fervently desire that our prayers accomplish victory in the spiritual warfare we attempt to wage on behalf of individuals and situations in our lives. Paul taught that the Holy Spirit Himself would come to our aid and bear us up in our weakness and inadequacy—coming to meet our supplication for help. Here again (just as shared through Jeremiah), we are encouraged by how God provides revelation and insight for us. We may not know what things God truly longs for us to seek in prayer, but His Holy Spirit is willing to intercede through us—even with "groanings too deep to be uttered" (beyond the understanding of our natural minds). And those prayers of the Spirit are in harmony with the will of God (see Romans 8: 26–27). They are destined to accomplish for His people astounding things—for His glory!

For I know the thoughts *and* plans that I have for you, says the Lord, thoughts *and* plans for welfare *and* peace, and not for evil, to give you hope in your final outcome. Then you will call upon Me, and you will come and pray to Me, and I will hear *and* heed you. Then you will seek me, inquire for *and* require Me [as a vital necessity] and find Me; when you search for Me with all your heart, I will be found by you, says the Lord, and I will release you from captivity. Jeremiah 29:11–14

The Terrible Disadvantage

There is a group of people on this earth who are the most disadvantaged of all people. It is not any of those who perhaps first come to our minds as "disadvantaged." It is the proud. The reason I make this statement is because if I am proud, then God is against me.

"God resists the proud," both Peter and James wrote, "But gives grace to the humble" (1 Peter 5:5 NKJV; see also James 4:6). God sets Himself against the proud—against the haughty, the insolent, the overbearing. He is against the disdainful and the scorners, against the presumptuous, arrogant, and boastful. He opposes and frustrates and defeats them. On the other hand, He continually gives grace (His favor and blessing) to the lowly of heart—those who are humble-minded enough to receive it. "For though the Lord is high, yet He has respect to the lowly [bringing them into fellowship with Him]; but the proud *and* haughty He knows *and* recognizes [only] at a distance" (Psalm 138:6).

A friend of mine, a very talented and extremely dedicated and conscientious new teacher, was recently challenged by an influential couple in the community where she teaches. They wanted their eight-year-old daughter (apparently quite spoiled at home) to be treated as the *prima donna* in her classroom as well. The father is a prominent lawyer and the mother is the president of the PTA—and it seems they quite confidently know how to throw their weight around. My friend, a sensitive and kindhearted woman, was naturally shaken and wounded by the harsh and unwarranted verbal assault from these proud and powerful people. She telephoned me and expressed her sense of perhaps not being able to "do this" teaching job.

Joni Eareckson Tada, a quadriplegic for over fifty years (ever since a diving accident when she was a teenager), has written she must face daily that she "can't do quadriplegia." However, she chooses to cry out to God, believing, "I can do all things through You as You strengthen me" (see Philippians 4:13). She is personally deeply convinced that rather than try to hide our need from God and others, a better way is to cast ourselves on the mercy of God and let Him show up through our weakness— since that is what He promises to do (see 2 Corinthians 12:9). She wrote the following about some "Christians" who feel they are so capable they have it all figured out (and therefore don't really need God).

Maybe the really handicapped people are the ones who wake up in the morning, hit the alarm, take a quick shower, scarf down breakfast, possibly give God a speedy tip-of-a-hat, and then zoom out the door on automatic cruise control. Like, "I accepted you as my Savior, Jesus, way back when. I put my sins on the counter in exchange for an asbestos-lined soul. I've got this Christian thing figured out. I'll check in with You now and then, but I can pretty much do it on my own." God says that if you live this way (proud), He's against you. The humble are the people who wake up in the morning knowing that they can't do this thing called life—not without the divine help of the Savior (and they are the ones to whom God will give grace). That makes my disability such an advantage. I'm so blessed to have it force me into the arms of Christ every morning—because I know that my human inclination is not to go to the cross every morning, but rather to turn my head on the pillow, and pull the covers up, and not face the day.[9]

So it seems after all that Joni (and also my friend—humbled by her recent experience in the teaching field and more than ever feeling her need of God's support and strength in her weakness) actually has an advantage over the proud and self-sufficient. The Scriptures teach an important principle that we can often inadvertently miss as we look at the events of our lives and those of lives around us. That principle is that the last line of the story is not written yet! From our present day-to-day perspective, it may appear the proud and arrogant prosper and get away with their insolent, disdainful ways and actions, that they are "happy" while the humble suffer and are trod upon (see Malachi 3:15). Asaph, a psalmist, also wondered, oftentimes with distress, about the prosperity of the proud and wicked compared with the frequent suffering of the righteous and humble (see Psalm 73). However, wise Solomon of old concluded that "Better is the end of a thing

---

9   Joni Eareckson Tada, "A Deeper Healing." Times Square Church
     message, 2016.

than the beginning of it, and the patient in spirit is better than the proud in spirit" (Ecclesiastes 7:8).

Recognizing this truth, we can discern the sensible and valid path of choosing to patiently and humbly wait on the all-seeing and all-wise Lord to "write the last chapter" of each person's life. There is Someone high above all He created who is in control of all things. It is written that to that One (who is the final authority) "everyone proud in heart *is* an abomination" (Proverbs 16:5 NKJV). There will surely come a day for every one of us when our "end" is clearly known. May I have determined long before then to have humbled myself beneath the mighty hand of God (see 1 Peter 5:6)—and be thus on the blessed side of His gracious favor. For in that day, the proud will assuredly be at an unmistakable and most terrible disadvantage!

"For there shall be a day of the Lord of hosts against all that is proud and haughty and against all that is lifted up, and it shall be brought low" (Isaiah 2:12).

"For behold, the day comes that shall burn as an oven; and all the proud *and* arrogant, yes, and all that do wickedly *and* are lawless shall be stubble; the day that comes shall burn them up, says the Lord of hosts" (Malachi 4:1).

"I will cause the arrogancy of the proud to cease" (Isaiah 13:11 KJV).

That Blessed Hope

Jesus came. And Jesus went. Thankfully, He is "the God who came!"

For long, trying centuries mankind looked for the One able to do for them what they could not do for themselves. All the human race groaned for redemption from the curse upon the earth and upon their lives. *When would the struggles be over? When would justice—right and good—prevail? When would there be peace instead of suffering? Did God care? Was He able (and was He willing) to override the bondage in which mankind was entangled and set him free?* Longing—longing for hope—they waited. Would He come?

Lo, I come, to do Thy will, O God. In the volume of the book it is written of Me ... Thou hast made ready a body for Me (see Psalm 40:7; Hebrews 10:4–7). Oh, unimaginable condescension: God Himself became a man! Because His children were of flesh and blood, He took on the same nature (see Hebrews 2:14). The Son of God (sent on a mission by the Father) humbled Himself—

down, down, down He lowered Himself and became one of us. He was to be called Immanuel: "God with us" (see Isaiah 7:14). "For unto us a Child is born, Unto us a Son is given; And the government will be upon His shoulder. And His name will be called Wonderful, Counselor, Mighty God, Everlasting Father, Prince of Peace. Of the increase of *His* government and peace *There will be* no end," (Isaiah 9: 6–7 NKJV).

Jesus (whose name means Savior) came to our earth to show us the Father. During the three years of His ministry He revealed God's nature to confused, questioning humanity. He demonstrated it was God's heart to restore to man what he had lost long ago in Eden by his own choice to rebel against the loving authority of his Maker. Jesus announced that "the acceptable year of the Lord" had arrived—when salvation and the free favor of God profusely abounded, available for all. He clearly stated His "job description" (prophesied centuries before): to preach good news to the meek and humble, to release the captives (physical and spiritual), to give recovery of sight to the blind and deliverance to those who were oppressed (downtrodden, crushed, bruised, and afflicted), to bind up and heal the brokenhearted and comfort all who mourn (see Isaiah 61:1; Luke 4:18). All these wondrous blessings were indeed to be greatly celebrated: "And it shall be said in that day, Lo, this is our God; we have waited for him, and he will save us: this is the Lord; we have waited for him, we will be glad and rejoice in his salvation" (Isaiah 25:9 KJV).

But there was more! Underlying and overarching these temporal benefits for people was the Son of God's grand mission to destroy the works of the devil. This adversary's evil intent toward humanity was a momentous part of the root cause of their desperate need for a Savior. The Son of God's predominant purpose in leaving His heavenly home and coming to earth was to die. "You have made ready a body for Me [to offer]" (Hebrews 10:5). God as Spirit could not die, but the God-man, Jesus (who took on the physical nature of human beings, who "came in the flesh") could suffer death. Why did the Son of God need to suffer death?

The day each human being is born, he falls under the long, fearful shadow of his inevitable death. Our enemy, Satan, keeps us in bondage to fear by holding this "wage of our sin" over our heads like an ever-threatening sword (see Romans 6:23). There is no one (no, not one) who has not sinned—who is not a sinner. Therefore, no one has an exemption from death (that is, from sin's wage, or consequence, of everlasting separation from God). There is no forgiveness of sin without the shedding of blood—in other words, there is neither release from sin and its guilt nor the remission of the due and merited punishment for sins (see Hebrews 9:22). The Law of God required this mark of the blood as a spiritual type—for indeed, apart from the shedding of the blood of the sinless One yet to come, Jesus Christ (the Messiah, the Sent One), there was no forgiveness of sins. The Son of God took on the body His Father had prepared for Him and came to earth to shed His own blood (to die) in our place. Oh, most stupendous and monumental substitution! "Herein is love, not that we loved God, but that He loved us, and sent His Son to be the propitiation for our sins" (1 John 4:10 KJV). Jesus did for us the greatest thing a man can do for his friends when He willingly laid down His life on our behalf—so we would not have to lay down ours (see John 15:13).

We who acknowledge and accept God's sacrifice of His only begotten Son's life in our stead by receiving that unparalleled, most holy gift are thereby freed from the death that is eternal (that is, the death of our spirit, which comes after the death of our body). "In accordance with this will [of God] we have been made holy (consecrated and sanctified) through the offering made once for all of the body of Jesus Christ . . . Whereas this One (Christ), after He had offered a single Sacrifice for our sins [that shall avail] for all time, sat down at the right hand of God" (Hebrews 10:10, 12).

When the devil saw Jesus die on the cross, he gleefully assumed he had permanently rid himself of the threat that God's Son was to his cruel dominion over man. But Satan missed something very significant and far reaching. Yes, Satan knows that legally all sinners are his lawful captives for he seduced them in the garden to rebel against God—and all rebels (sinners) must pay with their lives! "The wages of sin *is* death" (Romans 6:23 NKJV). But Satan is not omniscient (all-knowing), and what he decisively and critically did not know was that Jesus was not a lawful captive (see 1 Corinthians 2:7–8). Jesus never sinned; therefore, He did not deserve death as every other person does. Therefore, the grave could not hold Him! And by His resurrection from the sepulcher, the sinless Son of God demonstrated He had defeated death—for you and for me (for all who will believe and trust in Him as our substitute). "Because I live, you will live also" (John 14:19 NKJV).

After His world-changing resurrection, Jesus taught His followers for an additional forty days. Then He entrusted them with a very specific and impactful commission: to tell others all over the world, in all time, all that He had provided for them by His sacrifice. He told them that to be able to fulfill this weighty assignment, they would receive empowerment by the Holy Spirit, whom He would send to take His place. Then Jesus left the earth, ascending back to His Father. "So then the Lord Jesus, after He had spoken to them, was taken up into heaven and He sat down at the right hand of God" (Mark 16:19).

So is that the end of the story? Not at all! For He is coming again! Two angels present at the ascension of Jesus encouraged the disciples, "Men of Galilee, why do you stand gazing into heaven? This same Jesus, Who was caught away *and* lifted up from among you into heaven, will return in [just] the same way in which you saw Him go into heaven" (Acts: 1:11). Yes, the saga continues. Man's history on the earth has still other chapters ordained to occur. And the battle of the ages between God and Satan goes on (for a while yet). But this vastly pivotal war absolutely does have an end. And Jesus is already the Victor!

The complete and eternal consummation of His victory over God's enemy—and man's—will be fulfilled after Jesus's second coming to this sin weary earth. When that appointed time is, only the Father knows (see Matthew 24:36). But it is inexorably sure! And when He comes again, all the world shall know Him for who He is! Meanwhile, we who love Him are to occupy (do our assigned business) till He comes (see Luke 19:13). And so, with steadfast faith and trust in Him, we are patiently "awaiting *and* looking for the [fulfillment, the realization of our] blessed hope, even the glorious appearing of our great God and Savior Christ Jesus, the Messiah, the Anointed One, Who gave Himself on our behalf" (Titus 2:13–14).

Of Tremendous Gravity

Deep within the understanding of every man there is a consciousness of sin. Whatever men may want to label it, it is there—that sense of something not being right . . . that gnawing, discomforting thought that will not go away . . . that awareness within each individual there is some unnamed blockage between what he is and what he should be. Any religion that ignores this fundamental fact of the human spirit cannot truly meet man's need.

F.B. Meyer wrote, "To say with Buddha, 'You can wipe out your sins with good deeds,' or with Mohammed, 'God is good, and will not be hard on you,' is not enough."[10] The truthful and thoughtful human heart recognizes that sin must be dealt with radically and drastically. Jesus Christ has not treated sin lightly. He gave up His very life to loose men from the chains of its guilt and of its power.

---

10 F. B. Meyer, *Strength for the Day*, December 30 reading (Word Publishing, 1979).

The shed blood of Jesus, the Son of God, means that God has viewed our sin as being of tremendous gravity. To Him, it is no slight illness to be cured by a regimen of diet and exercise— nor even by countless good works we may do in an attempt to assuage our consciences. To Christ Jesus it is a condition that is so deep seated, radical, and perilous that it endangers the very fabric of our soul's health—as well as the scope of our soul's outlook on the future.

When we seek for answers to the burning spiritual questions of our hearts, there is a great danger in seeking answers in the wrong places. There are many false teachers and false leaders who realize very well that spiritual hunger in people (and a vacuum of spiritual truth) can make them vulnerable prey for these deceptive individuals' appealing "easy-way-out" deceptions—calculated to mislead. No such superficial and undemanding answers, however, can address our true spiritual needs. The desperate extremity of our spirits' plight cries out not for the unchallenging but for the substantial.

Such Clay!
Such a Potter!

*G*uess what! God does not love us because we are lovable. It's a nice thought (that we are really "somebodies," quite worthy of the sinless Son of God's dying on the cross to redeem us)—but it is an inaccurate assumption and a dangerous one! Why dangerous? Because if we mistakenly imagine He paid the price of His sacrifice because we were "worth it," we have no basis for the gratitude for His death on the cross that we rightfully ought to have. And one step further, this perverted belief of how valuable we are (because of how good we have made ourselves) lessens our appreciation of His love for us. We presume that we deserve His grace. But we don't! Sadly, our foundations will be laid terribly awry if we embrace this falsehood. We will not love God in truth if we do not accurately comprehend His love for us.

The truth is that the death of Jesus Christ in our place had nothing to do with our "worth"—but everything to do with the depths of our sin. It was in fact the extreme degree of our unworthiness that demanded the cost be so immeasurably high. The fact that God the Father gave His only begotten Son to die in our place—to meet the righteous demands of His holy justice—should not build our self-esteem! To the contrary, such an unfathomably great price should cause us to feel greatly ashamed for our sins that nailed Him to that cross. God did not give the life of His Son because we were "significant." Rather, this eternally matchless act was rooted in the love of His own heart—and was determined by only His goodness, mercy, and free grace.

There once was a woman who well knew her unworthiness, who accurately perceived the wretchedness of her own heart (even as the writer of the song "Amazing Grace" did when he expressed awe that such grace would "save a wretch like me"). She came to Jesus, seeing a quality in Him others in the same room that day did not perceive—and she fell at His feet in worship. She washed His feet with her tears of thankfulness for who she recognized and discerned He was—and for the totally unmerited love He, the holy Son of God, offered her. Jesus forgave her many sins and commended her for her much love (see Luke 7:47). He pointedly declared to the complacent, self-righteous Pharisee in that home (who had heartlessly given Him no respect or love—not even common courtesy) that it was because the Pharisee did not recognize his need for forgiveness that he had no love for Him. He who is forgiven little, loves little (see Luke 7:36–50). There is a marked correspondence. My gratitude that Jesus died for me is directly proportional to my realization of how sinful I am in God's eyes. To the extent I fabricate illusions of self-worth, my appreciation of His love for me remains shallow.

Deep within our hearts there may exist the knowledge of how unworthy we are—but our self-love makes it difficult to accept. Modern psychology, which touts self-esteem as our greatest need, is so popular because a part of us would rather love ourselves than love God! But the appeal of feeling good about ourselves can never fully erase from the memory embedded within the very core of our being that we are sinners—all guilty of rebellion against our Creator. If we never know our sinful, wretched unworthiness, then we will never know God's infinite greatness. We will not know Him as He really is—but only as a product of our imaginations, as a god we "create," and thus a false god, not the true God. And if we do not know ourselves and our God correctly, we will not genuinely love Him.

The infinite Creator, high and holy, offered His only Son to us—to unworthy sinners who had treated our Maker as our enemy, rejecting and defying Him. How could it be that at such an incomparable price He would stoop so low to redeem creatures who in essence wanted (like His adversary, Satan) to tear Him from His throne? We would rather deny His existence than bow to Him! And yet, His love paid the penalty on a tortuous cross for our awful affront to Him. And from that very cross, God's Son prayed that His Father forgive us who nailed Him there!

It is our recognition of the great chasm between our sinful unworthiness and the love revealed by what He did for us that awakens in us love and gratitude toward Him in return. When we have a clear vision of our own degraded hearts, and when we understand grace (unmerited favor), we will begin to have a clearer vision of God. The more unworthy we feel, the more grateful we will be for being so loved—for His having bridged the gulf between us, a gulf that was utterly impassable from our end. Appreciating His love, we will begin to love.

Love for God is not something we can produce by self-effort. And yet we are commanded to love Him! This, according to Jesus, is "*the* first and great commandment" (Matthew 22:38 NKJV). The knowledge of this directive and obligation is etched within every human conscience. And we are to love Him with our whole hearts—with all our being. This is not asked of us because God needs our love, for God lacks nothing; He does not need anything from us! It is certainly not to build His ego—for God is not proud or self-centered. It is in fact because of our own incorrigible self-centeredness that He commands us to love Him. Loving God is the one thing that can save us from our greatest enemy: self (that is, self-love). The commandment to love God is given for our own good! Pleasing God, our Maker, brings a high and lasting pleasure that our trying to please self facetiously promises to give—but never can. God does not force us to love Him—that would not be love. But if we desire Him, He promises that in seeking Him we will be rewarded—we will find Him (see Jeremiah 29:13; Hebrews 11:6). God loves us so much that He desires to give us the greatest blessing we could ever possess: Himself.

His love for us requires no reason (no cause or rationale)— for He loves without any reasons. Love is His very nature (see 1 John 4:8). Unlike His love, however, our love does require a reason. This is the basis, the grounds, for our love toward Him:

"We love Him because He first loved us" (1 John 4:19 NKJV). Just what does His love for us entail?

It is our rebellion against God's authority over us that in essence constitutes our sin. We have all thus sinned (see Romans 3:23). And man's sin is what has separated us from our Creator, that which has alienated us from divine fellowship—from our very source of eternal life (see Isaiah 59:1–2; Ephesians 2:1). In and of ourselves, we are totally incapable of appeasing God's righteous and justifiable wrath against our rebellion; we are hopelessly unequal to the task of satisfying His perfect justice. God Himself initiated the only means through which we can be reconciled to Him.

Pagan people make sacrifices to attempt to appease the anger of their gods (who, notably, despise humans), hoping that by their sacrifices they might change the gods' attitudes to be more favorably disposed toward them. However, our God (the only true God) loves sinful man. Paradoxically, while we were in sin (still choosing rebellion against Him), God's mercy and kindness toward us already looked upon us in loving favor (see Romans 5:6–8). Even before the foundation of the world (long before mankind existed, thus before man sinned), the Father and the Son already planned and made provision for the one single sacrifice that could make reparation for us sinners—that could turn away God's condemnation of our sin. He demonstrated His great love toward us by giving up His only begotten Son and sending Him to this earth. Jesus Christ willingly came into the world in human flesh and gave Himself to be the perfect sacrifice to pay the penalty (make atonement) for our sins (see Philippians 2:5–8; Hebrews 2:14–17).

Thus, God is the One who provided the sacrifice, the only sacrifice, that could be acceptable to reconcile man to Himself: "the Lamb slain from the foundation of the world" (Revelation 13:8 NKJV; see also 1 Peter 1:18–20). Only an infinite Being could bear for finite man the infinite penalty for our sin we all deserve, the penalty of condemnation in eternity (that is, eternal separation from God—the most devastating aspect of hell). This divine person, the sinless Son of God, became a man for our sakes. Being qualified by suffering as a human and fully experiencing all that we do, He became our High Priest— our needed Mediator between God and us—and He became our Savior (see Hebrews 2:10, 17; John 14:6). His blood (that is, His death) is the means for our being forgiven. It is His transcendent sacrifice—in Gethsemane and at Calvary—that is the life-giving spring, the source of our forgiveness.

He experienced death for every human being (in our place), but this sinless Man could not be held by death (as the wages of sin). In this glorious fact is our hope for salvation! By our faith in Jesus Christ as God's appointed sacrifice (the sacrifice that fully paid for our sins), we wayward, lost sinners can be reconciled to a holy God—we can return home to our Father's heart. And with our resurrected Savior, we will never die but are given to share with Him eternal life. This then is the wonderful gospel ("good news")—the gracious message of the provision made for us by the love of our God (see 1 John 4:9–10).

There is nothing so painfully grievous to the heart as love spurned or rejected. And there is no joy so deep as a response of love to love given. Would we want to be among those who turn their backs on God's love toward us? Could we disdain as nothing and cast aside as unwanted such radical and magnificent love? Oh, may we not give more sorrow—but rather profound joy—to the One who has so supremely demonstrated His love for us!

What a job we give our gracious Savior! He alone could do the wonderful work in us of saving us from ourselves. In all our misled thinking, He will right what is wrong. In all our erroneous doing, He will undo what is done amiss. In His great mercy, He will establish, strengthen, and prosper all within us that is right. He will both lead us out of despair for our failures and free us from our deadly pride—by His mighty power. Who would have such exceeding patience with mere dust of the ground, with such presumptuous and rebellious "clay" as we are? Ah, only so great and so tenderly loving and merciful a Potter would!

Behold the Man!

"*Behold the Man!*" (John 19:5 NKJV). Pilate spoke those words regarding Jesus as He stood before him in His crown of thorns—but Pilate did not know the depth of their significance. The name prophesied for Jesus by Isaiah hundreds of years before He was born was Immanuel, meaning "God is with us" or "God is one of us" (see Isaiah 7:14). The very Son of God became a man! Jesus, the Word of God—one with the Father, with Him from the beginning, the One by whom all things were created, and the very life and light of men (see John 1:1–5)—became a man, just like one of us created beings. Why would God so condescend? Why?

For the answer to that question, we must go very far back in our history—no, even farther back than history. Immeasurable ages before He created human beings, God (who alone is uncreated) created angelic beings—spiritual beings of great might, wisdom, and beauty. Because He gave these powerful, glorious beings free will, they could choose whether to serve Him. The most beautiful one of them all (the highest, wisest, and most gifted of all the angels) was named Lucifer ("brilliant, shining one"). He was given by God great authority, and he led heaven's worship of their Creator—that is, he did until the incalculably foreboding event occurred. Rebellion entered Lucifer's heart, and he decidedly chose to believe he could outshine God. His self-will asserted independence from God, and he (a created being) said, "I will ascend above God" (his Creator). His pride dared to presume he could supplant God's rule with his own—that he could take the place of "the Most High" (see Isaiah 14:12–21; Ezekiel 28:12–19).

Because he lifted himself up, wanting the glory (rightfully due only to God) for himself, he chose to become God's enemy. This prominent, lofty angel was no longer Lucifer ("perfect in beauty"), but in his iniquity, he became Satan ("adversary"). And from that point on, there was warfare in heaven. A third of the "stars of heavens" (angels) cast in their lot with Satan's rebellion. And God and His loyal angels fought with "the dragon and his angels" and cast them all out of heaven to the earth (see Revelation 12:4, 7–9; Luke 10:18; Ezekiel 28:16). To this day, this eternally consequential, radically far-reaching spiritual conflict continues among principalities and powers—between the hosts of heaven and the hordes of hell.

So what does all this have to do with man (with humankind) and with God Himself becoming a man? Of course, no created being could win in a battle against his Creator, so Satan is no match against God. God could squash that enemy in a second whenever He wanted to. But maybe He decided He would teach him a lesson first—get a message across to His adversary very clearly! One pastor put it this way: "God would demonstrate to Satan what He could do with a lesser being submitted to Him over a greater being not submitted to Him." Enter: man! God created man a little lower than the angels—and He gave man dominion to operate under His authority over the earth and everything in it (see Psalm 8:4–6). And there in Eden's garden, in the original state in which he was created, man walked with God—freely enjoying fellowship with his Creator with no barrier between them. Created in God's image as he was, man had been given free will like God has. God would not force anyone to be in relationship with Him—to love Him in return for His love (and trusting Him, to submit to obeying Him). Man would do so by choice. Or would he?

Satan had been cast out of heaven to earth and had lost his position and his authority. Now God had given man authority over planet earth. Aha! The opportunity to regain dominion! Thirsty for power, the adversary presumed that he would certainly "one up" God this time! The "greater" (a mighty, though fallen, angel) deceived the "lesser" (man) into disobeying God—that is, into coming out from under God's authority, rejecting God's rule over him.

Although God had given Adam and Eve innumerable trees in the garden from which they could freely eat, He had communicated only a single restriction to them: one solitary tree was off limits to them. God commanded them not to eat of the tree of the knowledge of good and evil and told them that if they did, they would surely die (see Genesis 2:16–17). "That serpent of old, called the Devil and Satan" (Revelation 12:9 NKJV), made his move—using his evil root of all temptations: "Don't believe what God said." Correspondingly, he also hissed the insinuation that God was trying to deprive them of something good: "God doesn't want you to eat that particular fruit because it will make you wise; your eyes will be opened, and you will be just like God, knowing good and evil." The deceiver also blatantly contradicted God (calling Him a liar), saying, "You will not surely die" (see Genesis 3:1–6).

And in seeking restricted knowledge, Adam and Eve lost their innocence—and much, much more. The desire to be wise enticed Eve as seeming quite reasonable, but hidden within that pleasant looking fruit was the seed of the great deception (and the very reason for Satan's fall): self-rule is better than being dependent on God. But God Himself was man's very source of life! Thus, by choosing independence from Him, Adam and Eve did indeed die (for death, in its most paramount sense, is separation from God). "The wages of sin *is* death" (Romans 6:23 NKJV). This consequence, significantly, is what man chose.

By Adam's one act of defiant disobedience to his Maker (and Owner), sin and its penalty, death, were brought upon not only Adam but by descent also upon the whole human race. And God's enemy, Satan, got what he wanted. When the first man chose to believe the adversary instead of trusting God, and when he submitted to the serpent instead of to God, Adam chose a new master—for whom we choose to obey is intrinsically our master (see Romans 6:16). With that momentous choice, Adam simultaneously gave his God-given authority over planet earth to his new master. Satan became the ruler over earth, the "prince of this world" (see John 14:30; Ephesians 2:2).

Mankind had rejected God. And by his rebellion against his Creator and life source, man became subject to death—the first death (of his physical body) and the second death later (the eternal separation of his spirit from God). By submitting to and obeying the devil, Adam and Eve gave him the right to hold them in bondage all their lives "through fear of death" (Hebrews 2:15 NKJV). Satan had won, after all. Man was now just his pawn. And as far as man's state was concerned, it seemed that God was defeated. Man was Satan's lawful captive—and Satan knew that God, being just by nature, would not break His own laws. God was holy, and He who did not justify or excuse rebellion and sin in Lucifer would definitely not excuse it in man. Man was lost to God forever! Apparently.

And so the ages rolled on—and on and on. Men could not return to Eden; they could not come back into that unbroken relationship with their Creator. And yet, eternity was in their hearts (see Ecclesiastes 3:11)—and a deep, undefined sense of a loss they could not name. That sense of loss was a longing for their Father, for their fatherland in His heart. But we human beings are captives—captives to sin and to self-will. Every child ever born has received the inheritance from Adam and Eve, our original parents, of the sin nature (a bent toward sinful rebellion against the authority of God . . . toward trusting in and relying on self rather than trusting God). We all have believed Satan's lie that we have a right to live for ourselves, to be our own god. The same thing that corrupted Satan's heart corrupted ours.

God's adversary certainly had us under his thumb! And the curse that sin had birthed infiltrated all the dwellers on earth—with its sorrow, regret, suffering, grief, pain, violence, misery, and evil. That curse (from our guilt) eroded all that was intended by God for good within humankind. The spiritual warfare outside of man (perpetually going on in the heavenlies among principalities and powers) was now reflected in a warfare inside of man. If he chose to attempt returning to a relationship with God through submission to His lawful reign and he strove to be what in his deepest spirit he knew he was created to be—try as he might, man could not sustain his effort (see Romans 7:18–19). Incessantly, man would slip and slide, stumble and fall. Even for the best of men, this inability engendered a deep restlessness within. Was there no way out—no way back? Was there anyone who could save man from this failure as his destiny? As much as he may struggle, a captive bound and chained cannot free himself!

The dilemma for every human being is that God's standard is too high for man to reach. No one can "be holy as I am holy" (see Leviticus 19:2; 1 Peter 1:16)—as is required to walk in fellowship with Him. Every human being is deeply flawed at the core and is unable to please God—to satisfy the demands of His Law, his moral absolutes (all of which are meant for man's good, to keep him safe). God's adversary knew this fact of man's incapability well and no doubt felt quite secure in his assumption that man would forever be subject to futility because of it. And so Satan could maliciously imprison him with cruel and relentless condemnation.

He knew the kingdom of God was based on law and that the requirements of that law would never change. Only if a man could satisfy the requirements of that standard would a way be opened for man to be reconciled to his Maker (be righteous before God and be restored into His favor). And no man could be capable of doing that—of making himself, by his own efforts, without sin, free of his inborn sin nature. It was impossible for man. There had never been a man for whom it was possible and there never would be, the devil smugly reasoned. The adversary, therefore, could endlessly keep all men his slaves. Satan's self-satisfied rationalization was that he ruled over man—and therefore God could not.

But there was a deep mystery (a secret knowledge known only to God, from before the earth and man were even created, from before the foundation of the world) that Satan knew nothing about (see 1 Corinthians 2: 7–8; Revelation 13:8: 1 Peter 1:20; Ephesians 1:4–9). Satan indeed is powerful and shrewdly cunning, but he is not omniscient. And this particular knowledge he missed was immense—grandly unprecedented and staggeringly consequential—and something he had in no way banked upon! This mystery was so significant that it was the beginning of the end of Satan's reign over man. The great Adversary was trumped—and would be eternally shamed and defeated! What was this hidden mystery of such phenomenal, incalculable worth? It was this: God Himself would become a man.

So now we see the answer to our original question: "Why did the Son of God so condescend as to become a man?" Because what was needed was a man! It was man who had given away his allegiance due to God and submitted to the enemy instead—and it was man who resultantly also forfeited his dominion over the earth. By Adam, death came to all men— for we are all members of his sinful race (and where sin is, death reigns). And the right, just, and holy requirements of God's Law had to be satisfied by a man—if mankind were ever to be legally reinstated into God's favor (able to be received by Him because of being rightly related to Him). In the new Man, Jesus Christ (the second Adam), all men who identified with and related to this Man could be made to live again—for this "last Adam" was a life-giving spirit (see 1 Corinthians 15:22, 45). With His coming, He began a new race of men.

Jesus, the very Son of God, who came in the flesh (who deliberately took upon Himself flesh and blood like those He now called His brethren), came to earth as a man under God's Law, just as we are. And He is the solitary, absolutely only human being who has ever or will ever fully obey God. Jesus Christ fulfilled all the Law of His Father perfectly, in every respect—both the letter of the Law and the spirit behind it, its essence—by all His actions and words, as well as by every internal motive of His heart. He was fully a man—and He was tried, tested, and tempted in every way we human beings are and experienced and identified with all our suffering, with complete fellow feeling. Yet, unlike every one of us, this Man never sinned (see Hebrews 4:15).

Therefore, when Satan took hold of Jesus and subjected Him to death as the punishment for sin, he illegally stepped over the line. This man—Jesus Christ, Son of Man—was not a lawful captive! Jesus was sinless. Therefore, death had no rights over Him. Thus, the grave could not hold Him! The resurrection of Jesus from the dead proved that He was sinless. It was God's complete attestation to that fact. And it was also the Father's vindication of Jesus for who Jesus said He was—the Son of God, and as a pure and holy sacrifice to atone for sin, wholly acceptable to Him (see Romans 1:4). And it is this Jesus, this holy God-Man, who submitted to death on behalf of all of us as our substitute. He offered up Himself to His Father to satisfy the righteous demands of God's standard of obedience—and God's justice due to us all for not meeting His standards. By going through death, this one Man destroyed once and for all the power of death over mankind (see Hebrews 2:14).

Satan trembles at the words "the Son of God, who came in the flesh" (see John 6:51; Galatians 4:4). He hates the name of Jesus—"Son of Man." Why? Because Satan abhors the fact that he was overthrown by a man! Our enemy never supposed it could be possible, for he self-confidently and pompously presumed there could never, ever be a man without sin. Satan had been given the dominion he coveted over earth by man. It had to be a man to take it away from him! And indeed, another man, the second Adam, the very Son of God incarnate did just that—forever defeating the devil and his hordes of demons.

And now, when we human beings surrender—when we accept and confess in humility that we are too weak, too desperately incapable by our own efforts to please God (to meet His high standard, to fully keep His wise and holy decrees)—it is then that our real life can begin for us. When we deeply realize how our own human nature will always be opposed to God's reign over us, then we will finally be on the verge of comprehending that our most imperative, life-and-death need is a new nature (a new and completely different heart, mind, and will—

indeed, a new spirit) (see Ezekiel 36:25–27). Thankfully, God's boundless mercy and His wondrous grace have made a way, opened a door for us to truly live again—in the most profound sense of the word. By the offering up of His own sinless Son, the Father has reconciled us to Himself. Through our union with Jesus Christ, God receives us into His favor again—so we can live before God in unbroken fellowship with Him.

By my being joined with the Son of Man (by faith in what He accomplished on that cross for my sake, in my place), I can die to my own struggling efforts to pursue His will for me of right living and right being. Through earnestly embracing in my heart the atoning sacrifice of God's own sinless Son to pay for my sin, I can receive forgiveness of all my failures toward Him—and complete remission of my sin. At the same time, through the perfect righteousness of Jesus (which amazingly the Father lovingly imputes to me), I can be declared in right standing again with my God. The miracle of miracles!

Since the grave could not hold Jesus (and because He lives), we who have identified with His death can be identified with Him in His resurrection also—we can be raised to a new quality of life with Him (see John 14:19; Romans 6:6–11). The very Spirit who raised Jesus from the dead is given to us (see Ephesians 1:19–29; Romans 8:11–15). The Spirit of Jesus Himself comes to live in you and me—giving us the ability to fully trust our Father and consequently enabling us to obey Him just as Jesus did. The Son of Man not only paid the penalty of human sin, but He also broke the bondage of the serpent's grip on us that had held us hopelessly enslaved to the dictates and rule of sin (see Hebrews 2:14). Death as the wage of our sin is a vanquished foe that can no longer intimidate us. For in giving

His own life to us, our Redeemer provided a force within our lives to dominate death in all its manifestations. Jesus gives us the victory—even His own victory (see 1 Corinthians 15:55–57)!

The uncreated, eternal God descended into His creation—and into human nature (the natural). And when He rose again, He brought human nature up with Him into heaven (and into the supernatural). Jesus, the Son of God, was a man from Mary's womb to the tomb in the garden near Golgotha's cross. If He had been only a man, He would have been just another martyr who died for a good cause. But because he was fully God and fully man (God incarnate)—and because as a human He defeated sin and death and entered back into the glory He had with His Father before the world was (see John 17:5)—in Him all humanity has hope for eternal life.

Yes, mere man, weak man—when united to the God-Man—can be more than a conqueror over sin, death, and Satan (see Romans 8:37). This is the triumphant and wonderful newness of life that the Son of Man, the second Adam, left His home with His Father in heaven and came to this earth to bring us: the freedom at long last for man to be able to obey his God through "a new spirit" (that wholeheartedly trusts in His love). Having been reconciled to God, brought back into harmony with our Maker, through the death and the resurrection power of the Man Christ Jesus, you and I can realize "the hope of His calling" (Ephesians 1:18 NKJV)—the high, holy, and incomparably blessed destiny God has for us. This is Eden regained. "Behold the Man," yes—and worship Him!

A New Humanity

By the cross of Jesus, the righteous decrees of God against us (foundationally, for our rejection of His authority over us as our Creator) were abolished. Jesus fulfilled God's Law for mankind perfectly—not for Himself, but for us. By His solitarily sinless life, Jesus Christ met and satisfied the Law's holy demands on all of humankind—such that the Law had no more claims it could ask. By His own crucified flesh as He offered Himself as our substitute for the punishment we deserved (eternal separation from God, our Father), the enmity between God and us that had resulted from our rebellion was annulled. The hostile dividing wall between man and his Maker was broken.

Additionally, dividing walls between men were broken down. The apostle Paul wrote that Jesus Christ did this so "He from the two might create in Himself one new man" (Ephesians 2:15). Thereafter, both Jew and Gentile (people other than Jews—from every nation, kindred, people group, and tongue) reconciled to God through the death of His Son could be united in a single body by means of His cross.

In His resurrection, Jesus has constituted the origin and head of a new race, a new quality of humanity: the race of regenerate men. All who believe in Him are born into that new humanity—a race of people who are recipients of His resurrection life and power. This "new man" (versus "the old man"—the merely human) is now made of two intertwined lives: the human life and the life of the risen Son of God.

Originally we were created in God's image, in His likeness—and in the blessed nature of the Son of His love, who was His "fellow" (see Genesis 1:28; Zechariah 13:7). But in Adam's fall, all of us human beings (who descend from Adam and thus share the propensity toward sin that ran through Adam's nature) fell from that original type. We greatly marred that image in ourselves—and to a tragically indescribable degree, lost it.

Through His death on the cross, Jesus Christ restored to us what we were created to be. We who believe in and receive the atoning sacrifice of the Son of God on our behalf (trusting in His taking the guilt of our sin upon Himself) shall again be made like Him—fully in His image. The atonement provided by the sacrifice of the Lamb of God having purged the iniquity out of our hearts, when we then receive His righteousness to be our own, we can be reconciled to the Father (brought back into harmony with Him and received into His favor). We are made a child of God. Jesus said, "I ascend unto my Father, and your Father" (John 20:17 KJV). We shall once more know the ineffable pleasure of the fellowship of like natures—of oneness with our God. Through Jesus, we can again be where we belong.

SECTION III

—◆—

The Journey Onward

Looking at
Peter's Waves

I struggle with keeping my eyes where I need to in order to run the race of life that is set before me. Thankfully, Paul gave us wise direction as to how to run our race (see Hebrews 12:1–3). (By the way, my race is different from yours, and your race is not like mine. We each are given our own unique race—custom designed for each one of us by our all-wise, loving Father God.)

How then do I run my race? How do I hang in there when the going gets so extremely rough? How do I persevere to the end when there seems never to be an end to the weary struggle—and I wonder if I'm just spinning my wheels? The apostle Paul taught the method to succeed in this running is by "looking unto Jesus."

My eyes and my thoughts are naturally drawn to the circumstances around me that are affecting me. This is a normal tendency built into human beings. However, it is not the way to be able to run the race—to live my life as my higher nature desires to. For that, I must go beyond normal and natural, and I must move into the supernatural. And to do that, I need to change my focus. Anything I accomplish in life (or fail to accomplish) depends on where I fix my focus.

It was a dark, stormy night on the Sea of Galilee. The disciples of Jesus were in their boat in the middle of the lake, fighting with great difficulty against the winds hindering them from being able to make progress in their struggle to go to the other side. They had left Jesus miles back on the other shore because He had wanted to go up to a mountain to pray and be alone with His Father. It was in that drowsy, hypnotic time of night between three and six in the morning when the exhausted disciples saw what appeared to them to be a ghost walking toward them on the surface of the water. They were stupefied and terrified! But it was Jesus—doing something they had never seen Him do before! "It is I. Be not afraid," He encouraged them. We remember the story. Peter responded to this amazing revelation by asking Jesus to bid him to walk on the water to Him, and Jesus said, "Come." And sure enough, Peter also walked on the water—that is, until he changed his focus. When he looked at the boisterous wind (instead of keeping his gaze on Jesus), Peter began to sink. And so will we (see Matthew 14:24-31).

I have a situation in my family life that continues after many years, bringing me much heartache. Things will seem for a little while as though they are going to improve, and then another crisis arises—and down into a battle with depression I find myself sinking. But the gracious Holy Spirit has been working on me, patiently teaching me (despite my often being a slow learner). As a child of God, there assuredly is provision for me not to have to experience extreme mood swings according to my circumstances. Instead, it is possible for me to learn to appropriate all the aspects of victory Jesus provided for me by His death on the cross. The more I learn to apply the certainty of those truths to my efforts to run my race, the more I can live on an entirely new level of life. Also, as I grow in my ability to hear the Master speaking "It is I" amid the very circumstances troubling me, those powerful words will increasingly stabilize my faith in Him. I will be brought to securely rest in the One who will surely calm my inner storms (at the time when His wisdom and love chooses is for my highest good).

In the natural, my mood may be dictated by the way things appear. When things look good, I go to the "heights," but when things look bad, I go to the "depths." However, if I determinedly fix my eyes (and, above all, my trust) on Jesus, my emotions will no longer be ruled by appearances. Looking unto Jesus, I will be held steady. Beholding, as it were, His face (seeing the love in His eyes for me—yes, even me, and getting a glimpse of the flames of fire in those eyes—flames of glorious almightiness and pure holiness), something changes for me. I thereby get positioned where I need to be: in a higher reality than is visible around me. No longer walking by sight but now walking by faith, I am able to realize more clearly that those heights and depths that have kept me on an emotional roller-coaster way too long are already taken care of! Jesus has dealt with them for my sake, and the painful fluctuations can be altogether over for me.

My faithful teacher, the Holy Spirit, recently quickened to me this freeing truth that God showed Paul: "For I am persuaded that neither death nor life, nor angels nor principalities nor powers, nor things present nor things to come, nor height nor depth, nor any other created thing, shall be able to separate us from the love of God which is in Christ Jesus our Lord" (Romans 8:38–39 NKJV). Neither my "highs" nor my "lows" truly have the capacity to separate me from my source of life eternal.

Where then will I focus? Will I allow my attention to be concentrated on the waves, grown tempestuous and threatening? Or will my focal point be the Lord Jesus Christ— on Him whom even the winds and the sea obey (see Matthew 8:27). Will I determinedly remember that this Jesus, by whom all things were created, is absolute Master of all things (see Colossians 1:16)? Faith in Jesus allowed Peter to walk on the waves; it was like a life buoy holding him up. Unbelief sent him down. With God's ever-present help, may we choose no longer to look at "Peter's waves" that would swallow us up but instead to look at Jesus—and walk with Him above those very waves! Maintaining that focus will keep my heart enfolded in His peace beyond understanding (see Philippians 4:6–7). Keeping my eyes on Jesus, I can be safely anchored in an eternal reality—far beyond the mere appearance of things to my natural perspective. "Thou wilt keep him in perfect peace, whose mind is stayed on thee" (Isaiah 26:3 KJV).

Standing above the Maze

A story is told of a telephone operator years ago who received a call every day from the same man, asking for the time of day. After a few weeks of this, she asked him why he was asking her for the time. "To set my watch," he said, "because I have to blow the whistle at my factory every day at exactly noon." To his surprise, the woman replied, "Oh, my! I set my watch every day by that whistle signal!" We may laugh, amused at this incident. Yet considering the bafflement of them both as they realized the lack of certainty of what they each had presumed was a sure standard, we ourselves may be taught a lesson.

This could be a picture of our world today. More and more, people are realizing they have built a sense of security on false foundations. Despite theories and views of life that seemed to have worked for us in the past, newer ideologies, supposedly advanced world views, may leave us feeling bankrupt. Why? Because many of the opinions and answers other men are now offering us have deviated from a safe standard (just as the whistle signal deviated from the true time). And we are left without any objective standard. Resultantly, we have been bequeathed an undercurrent of insecurity and discontentment that is running rampant beneath the surface of our lives. Many of us may have even lost confidence that there is any such thing as a future for the human race.

Archimedes was a Greek mathematician, physicist, engineer, and inventor who is considered one of the greatest scientists of classical antiquity. He was the first to explain the principle of levers, and he is remembered for an assertion regarding having a lever long enough to move even the earth. The key was having a fulcrum for his lever that was outside the earth. And, indeed, that is just what human beings need!

Actually, we have "Archimedes's fulcrum." We have an objective standard that is from outside our world (and because it is not from ourselves, not from our earth itself, it is not susceptible to deviation from the winds of time). Indeed, it is from outside of time, from beyond time's boundaries. It is in fact timeless. It is the fulcrum that alone can bring balance to the levers of our attempts to understand this complex phenomenon called life. It is the Word of God.

A valuably insightful quote has anchored my boat as it tosses on the sea of life's uncertainties: "The man who stands above the maze can direct you through all its labyrinth by the readiest path."[11] God is that One who stands above the maze. As our Creator, He is the only one who has the big picture. F. B. Meyer wrote, "God, who made you for your life, and your life

---

11   F. B. Meyer, *Strength for the Day* (Word Publishing, 1987), January 10 reading.

for you, can direct you—and He only."[12] Our path will certainly open clearly before us when we learn to "lean not on your own understanding" but rather to "in all your ways acknowledge Him" (Proverbs 3:5–6 NKJV). When we no longer look down merely onto our path (or around at others) but simply look upward into the face of Christ, we will assuredly find that He is utterly trustworthy to be our guide.

And, yes, the eternal Word of God assures us there is indeed a future for mankind. "Eye has not seen, nor ear heard, Nor have entered into the heart of man the things which God has prepared for those who love Him" (1 Corinthians 2:9 NKJV). If it is my heart's true desire to please Him, then this promise is my immutable and delightful certainty.

---

12   Ibid.

Where Is My Focus?

I felt as though the ground under my feet had turned to water—and I was sinking. I couldn't find a solid rock on which to stand. The waters of problems too big for me to handle swirled around my feet, then rose up around my knees, then higher, and higher. No safety rope of any possible solution was thrown to me. Nowhere could I see a life-preserver of hope for some way out. The horizon all around my spot of sinking was gray—just stormy waves and relentless winds. All seemed against me. I would drown. I would surely drown!

Then came a voice: "Look up!" And again, "Look up!" From out of the dark night around me, a voice I recognized called to the panic of my heart, "You are looking at the wind and at the waves." The calming voice continued, "Instead, look at Me."

Suddenly I saw a different scene. I looked on a man beside a wooden fishing boat on a rough sea, and he seemed to be trying to walk on top of the water. But just as I had felt I was doing, he was sinking down to his knees into the deep. Yet less than a dozen feet away from him, another man stood serenely on the surface of the water, which was as still as glass under Him. His face was full of a deep peace. His strong arm was outstretched toward the first man, and somehow I knew that the man struggling in the water would be lifted up.

So much depends on where we look! As long as Peter, that fisherman of long ago, looked into the face of Jesus, things were possible for him that he could never do on his own in his natural human ability. And the same is true for us. As I contemplated this, the Lord gave me to see that my problems and difficulties are like the waves of a stormy sea. If I choose to focus on them, they can overwhelm me—and I may sink beneath the weight of them. But there is Someone who is Master of the sea (and indeed of all creation—for it was every bit made by Him)! It is just a small thing to Him that wind and waves obey Him.

This mighty Creator, in gentle condescension and tenderness, nudged my fearful heart with a question: "Am I able to make your challenges and crises obey Me too?" I at once felt encouraged and convinced of the reality that if I would keep my eyes on Him (focusing on who He is, on His nature, and on His character), then my worry and fear could be calmed—and could melt away at His word. This One whom the wind and waves obey (see Mark 4:37–41) is able indeed to take care of me—and it is His gracious desire to do so!

We are weak creatures. We cannot make our next breath come or command our heart to beat. All of us are susceptible to anxiety—and beyond that, to despair. In all lives there are periods of storm and tumult. Stress and trouble are part of the lives of everyone on the globe in one form or another. And we will very likely experience more and more difficult, distressing, even perilous occurrences in our personal lives and all around us in the future. Will we then become disquieted and deeply unsettled in our spirits—perhaps afraid and terrified to the point of being plagued by torment? I am learning that it does not have to be so.

Amid the gales and tempests of life surging around us, it is possible to find peace. Our hearts can become anchored steadfastly—despite crashing waves, shifting sands, and violent winds. "I have told you these things so that in Me you may have perfect peace *and* confidence. In the world you have tribulation *and* trials *and* distress *and* frustration; but be of good cheer—take courage, be confident, certain, undaunted—for I have overcome the world.—I have deprived it of power to harm, have conquered it [for you]" (John 16:33). An unfading peace (the very peace of Jesus Himself) that transcends all our understanding and overarches beyond circumstances can guard our hearts—when we fix our eyes and our minds on Him, the Prince of Peace (see John 14:27; Isaiah 26:3; Philippians 4:6–7). When we decisively set our trust in Him (who is the victorious Conqueror on our behalf), He will enable us to walk on top of the tumultuous waters—with Him!

At this very moment you may be passing through a storm of trouble, trying to navigate through seas of great difficulty. Angry billows of calamity, one after another, may seem to beat upon you until it seems the little boat of your life will surely be overwhelmed. Will you ever reach a harbor of safety and rest? Although God may allow us to pass through storms of trial for reasons not evident to us while in the midst of them, one thing is certain: He provides an anchor for our souls. Faith cleaves its way through the darkness and the driving clouds of mist, and it firmly grasps hold of the hand of the eternal Father. In His presence is our shelter, our refuge. Look up to your God—and cry to Him who holds the winds in His fist, the waters in the hollow of His hand (see Proverbs 30:4; Isaiah 40:12). He sees you. He will not forsake those who cry to Him; He will not allow you to be engulfed!

No one asks for the storms of life, but everyone encounters them. Importantly, the problems and hardships of life can press us into faith. If we had no difficulties, we would have fewer opportunities to learn the vital reality that we can indeed trust God. Could it be that God has permitted my trial just to show me how He can deliver me out of it? But one may ask, "How can I persevere when the storms drive so hard and relentlessly?" We can persevere (and not fall into dismay, not give up) by facing the storms with the promises of God. "When you pass through the waters, I *will be* with you; And through the rivers, they shall not overflow you" (Isaiah 43:2 NKJV). My faith can grow more and more unshakeable as I believe Jesus is in the storm with me—and that He will see me through it. He can easily carry me in His arms through the waters or He can lift me above the storm's power to harm me. He will either calm the storm or He will calm me.

Significantly, my committing to persevere through the storm may be the very thing necessary for the character of my God to be more deeply revealed to me. There are things He can tell us—and inward peace He can give us—only through storms. "Only when Christ opened thine ear to the storm did He open thine ear to the stillness."[13] The storm may be His ordained occasion for my "faith muscle" to be strengthened—as I learn how to cast my care on Him and then see how He indeed does take care of me (that truly, God never fails). Charles Spurgeon, familiar in his own life with many despairing troubles, wrote, "In the depth of troubles we learn the sufficiency of grace. . . . Young men do not become midshipmen altogether through going to school; they must go out to sea. We must do business in great waters; we must be really on the deck in a storm, if we would see the works of the Lord and His wonders in the deep. . . . Conflicts bring experience, and experience brings that growth in grace which is not attained by any other means."[14] Through our trials we learn the profitable lesson of how ample His provision of grace is—and we prove the triumph of His grace. Above all, trials can strengthen our trust in God (in His love for us individually—and in His wisdom, goodness, and power). And in the future on our earthly pilgrimage, trust in Him is the most essential thing we will need.

So carry on bravely, brothers and sisters, for "indeed we count them blessed who endure. You have heard of the perseverance of Job and seen the end *intended by* the Lord—that the Lord is very compassionate and merciful" (James 5:11 NKJV). This is the Father-heart of God. He feels our pain with us—and He submits us to the refiner's fire only to bless us through it. Just as He did for Job (after all the anguish, sorrow, and

---

13 George Matheson, *Springs in the Valley*, quoted from Mrs. Charles Cowman (Zondervan Publishing, 1968) June 6 reading.

14 Charles Spurgeon, *Gleanings Among the Sheaves* (Baker Book House, 1977) 56.

bewilderment), He has an outcome of mercy and compassion planned for you through all you have suffered. Only take on this one task as yours for now: focus on your heavenly Father's heart, so full of compassion—and always one with us in our affliction (see Isaiah 63:9).

Also, it is vitally important to be aware that if you focus on yourself and your difficulties, you are entering dangerous territory. That is where the enemy wants us to focus—so he can distort reality and can inject thoughts of discouragement into our minds. If you move into that forbidden territory, he can easily lasso you there and drag your thoughts further downward into despair. His strategy has always been to magnify the problem and to try to minimize our perception of God's greatness and faithfulness (already proven so many times to us). Remember, though: God is greater than any Goliath! Look up (and away from the wind and waves)— and take the hand that our Victor Jesus this very moment is extending to you. He will always help His child who calls upon Him in his distress (see Psalm 107:13–14).

No crisis can swallow us who believe in Jesus—for there is absolutely nothing that can separate us from the love of the One who gave His very life to redeem us (see Romans 8:35–39). In times of suffering, adversity, pain, and perplexity, when fear and confusion try to overwhelm and flood our hearts, if we will earnestly remember His everlasting love for us (and focus on the truth of His plans of eternal good for us), we can be enabled to become more than conquerors—even in the very teeth of our problem. For beyond the limited reasonings of our minds (and the battered, undependable emotions of our souls), our wills can choose to take their stand on the solid-ground truth that our God is on His throne. And that He is in control. And above all, our hearts have the capacity to choose to believe He is trustworthy. And it is as we thus believe that we will see how He will fight for us (see 2 Chronicles 20:12–17)!

Even when everything seems to be changing all around us from what we have known, we can be fortified in our spirits by knowing our God never changes. We may be perplexed, but He is not. There is only one Rock on which to stand when dark clouds gather and waters of turbulence menacingly roar. That firm foundation is our God's sovereignty. Neither human confusion nor anarchy annihilates His throne. And no enemy power can ever snatch the scepter from His hand. Our God lives, and He is in control. Because our God reigns (in justice and in righteousness), He will bring good out of turmoil and calamity. Even as springs can be unsealed by the upheaval of an earthquake, hope and grace will rise up for His people from the apparent uncertainty and mayhem of troubling times.

Increasingly, everywhere we look it may seem chaos is reigning. But God's Word and His promises remain firmly sure. However severe the storm that is yet to sweep over the earth, that which God has said will come to pass surely will come to pass (see Isaiah 55:11). Regarding the time of distress, tribulation, and anguish that is certainly coming on all the earth, Jesus said, "Now when these things begin to happen, look up and lift up your heads, because your redemption draws near" (Luke 21:28 NKJV). Thus, we are called to understand that the time of great trouble on earth for all mankind is only a prelude to the glorious consummation of God's good and perfect plan for our eternity in His presence.

By lifting our gaze upward (not looking merely around us), we will be able to see past the ordeal—and to perceive the wonderful threshold on which we stand. Lifting our heads up from hanging down in fear and despair—and instead looking unto Jesus (into His face)—we will be given to see that no storm is powerful enough to prevent Him from accomplishing His will. Concentrating our attention on what we have in Him and are in Him (and what He has so lovingly prepared for us), we can overcome all fear. We can be filled instead with praise and exceeding joy in our blessed expectation of His great faithfulness.

Where is your focus? On the wind and waves? Or on Him whom the wind and waves must obey?

We Can't Live Without Oxygen

Keeping Hope Alive

*H*ow *can we keep hope alive in such a world as we live in?* God wants his people able to abound in hope—to be buoyant and triumphant. But we are often surrounded in life by awful and merciless forces that seem they may overwhelm us at any moment. Although we try to remain hopeful, our hope may be undermined by depression stemming from disappointed plans or dreams, poverty or failing health, betrayal in relationships or cruel ingratitude, slighted love or deep loneliness. These and innumerable more circumstances flood over us like a hurricane that threatens to sweep us away and drown us.

Perhaps we have had seasons of spiritual refreshing when gratefully the waste places in our lives have begun to become as fruitful fields. But then it seems that the tide of blessing recedes, and the forces of evil pour over us again—and another battle with our foes must be fought. Is abounding in hope possible in such a world? I believe it is! But there is only one way it is possible: by the power of the Holy Spirit. The apostle Paul prayed that the power of the Holy Spirit would fill the Romans with hope (see Romans 15:13). If we do our part by focusing on eternal things and taking our eyes off temporary circumstances, choosing to take a resolute stand on His Word, this power of God's Holy Spirit will never fail us.

Yes, life can be like a labyrinth. We wonder if we will ever find our way through it. Life is a riddle; even the world's greatest thinkers and wisest philosophers have not been able to solve the problems ever present with us of evil, pain, suffering, and death. However, there is One, whose name is "Counselor" (Isaiah 9:6 NKJV), who assuredly can resolve the riddles that plague us. As we learn to come to Him (and to align our lives with His ways), we can find rest through trusting Him (see Matthew 11:28–29). Our trust in Him will never be disappointed—for He is the One in whom "are hidden all the treasures of wisdom and knowledge" (Colossians 2:3 NKJV).

Notably, we can inadvertently open a door for the enemy to siphon off our hope (and also our joy) by fixing our eyes in the wrong place. For example, we may strain our poor, weak eyes trying to look into the future (presumably so we can control it). But Jesus commanded us to leave our future in God's hands, without any anxious thought on our part, but trusting Him with it (see Matthew 6:34). Our very anxiety itself (our worries, fears, and murmuring as we doubt our Father's loving care for us) can actually precipitate the undesired consequence of our walking right into the jaws of trouble. Such a focus tends to produce a condition that ironically brings the very things we fear onto us—sometimes like an avalanche (see Job 3:25)! Simply put, we cannot worry and trust at the same time. Worry robs us of trust. And a lack of trust in God positions us dangerously in a state of vulnerability to our enemy's malicious ploys and schemes.

To remain spiritually strong and healthy we need to live in a sustained atmosphere of trusting God. If we have the right foundation of trust, it follows that we will build praise to our trustworthy Father (as well as thanksgiving) onto that foundation—and our lives will be as an edifice that will stand. It is a vital spiritual truth that our praise to God sets up a mantle of protection that insulates us from our adversary. Not only does praising and being thankful to God clothe us in divine protection but choosing to make it a lifestyle enlarges us spiritually. This enlargement comes as we are enabled to see all that is happening in our lives and around us from a different perspective—a higher, more accurate, and truer viewpoint.

Our bodies can live a little while without food and water, but oxygen is something we must have all the time to survive. One pastor wrote that praise and thanksgiving to God are like the believer's very breath—that they are our spiritual oxygen! To be survivors, and to endure to the end (see Matthew 24:13), we need to lift our hearts in thanksgiving and worship continually. And as we thus bless our God, our lives will surely be lifted to a new level of living. Our hope will grow, and thrive, and be sustained—as we trust in and appreciate Him. He of whom it is written that "the government shall be upon His shoulder" (Isaiah 9:6 KJV) is absolutely worthy of our trust!

The Favoring Breezes
of Adversity

Ease does not produced greatness. Rather, the truly greatest helpers of humanity have learned their lessons in the school of suffering. It is through struggles, pain, and loneliness they have won their character—the kind of character that has made a difference for the better not only in their own lives but also in the lives of those around them. They are the great "victor souls." They are those who perceived that the best, most worthy things in life lie beyond some battlefield. And they were willing to fight their way across that thunder-scarred plain to obtain them.

These were the people of high natures, and because of that, they had come to understand there are blessings we cannot obtain if we will not accept and endure suffering. In the same way we cannot expect a harvest until after the plowshare has done its work, there are gifts and revelations from God to benefit our lives that can come to us only through sorrow. It is written of the very greatest character of all time (the One around whom all destiny revolves) that even He could be "made perfect" (that is, completely made as a Man like us—fully equipped and qualified through experience to empathize with us as human beings—and thus to be our interceding High Priest and Savior) only through suffering (see Hebrews 2:10). If suffering was thus chosen for Jesus, the very Son of God in the flesh, then is it not probable that it is a chosen means for completing us also? There must be a very high treasure, indeed, hidden within the rough wrapping of this thing called suffering—surely an invaluable treasure not to be missed.

Apparent adversity, then, can turn out to be for our advantage. May we picture for a moment the majestic eagle rising against a strong headwind? Friend, his victorious rising is not *despite* the wind but *because* of it! If faced at just the right angle, the opposing force becomes a lifting force.

It is true that the environment of a blasting storm buffets the ship, tears its rigging, scars its bulwarks. But it is likewise true that it can make the hands of the voyagers strong, their hearts brave, and their soul's sinews robust in a way the calm seas never could. And so, true heart, fellow traveler on life's wide sea, may you take courage—and spread your sails to the favoring breezes of adversity!

The tears we shed are not in vain;
Nor worthless is the heavy strife;
If, like the buried seed of grain,
They rise to renovated life.

It is through tears our spirits grow;
'Tis in the tempest souls expand,
If it but teaches us to go
To Him who holds it in His hand.
Oh, welcome, then, the stormy blast!
Oh, welcome, then, the ocean's roar!
Ye only drive more sure and fast
Our trembling bark to heaven's bright shore.[15]

Thomas C. Upham

---

15   The Christian's Daily Challenge (Harvey Christian Publishers Inc., 1954) 316.

Floating Iron

Inevitably we will all face impossible situations in our lives. Heavy and very serious matters will weigh upon us—and despite all our best efforts, solving our dilemmas will seem hopeless.

There is a story from days of old of an occurrence in the life of the prophet Elisha. He was accompanying friends, sons of the prophets, as they cut down trees for beams to build a dwelling place. As one of the men chopped, his axe-head came loose and fell into the nearby water. He was especially concerned and dismayed because the axe-head was borrowed. As a man of God, he felt that having borrowed something to do God's work, his losing it would put the name of His God at the risk of being dishonored. His "Alas!" came to Elisha's ears, and what did God do? He prompted His servant Elisha to perform the seemingly unrelated act of tossing a stick into the water—just above where the axe-head had sunk. And the account reads, "The iron did swim" (2 Kings 6:6 KJV). This God—who can make iron rise to the surface of water and float—is our God!

What hopeless difficulty grieves your heart today, child of God? Is it financial straits that press unceasingly on you every way you turn? Is it a work you feel led by God to undertake but seems absurdly beyond your strength or ability? Is it the severe sorrow and lonely ordeal of a loved one's excruciating suffering—about which you can do nothing? Is it an agonizing battle within yourself against the stubborn wickedness of the "old Adam" that will not relent to the higher desires of the "new man"?

The God of the prophets still lives to help His cherished children. Jesus yearns for us to profoundly grasp that "all things *are* possible to him who believes" (Mark 9:23 NKJV). When two blind men came to Him, pleading He have pity on them, Jesus simply asked them if they believed He was able to give them their sight. In response to their "Yes, Lord," He touched their eyes and said to them, "According to your faith *and* trust *and* reliance [on the power invested in Me] be it done to you" (see Matthew 9:27–30).

Struggling one, seek the Lord this day. Bring your desperation to Him. Your impossibility is an opportunity for your Father God to show Himself strong on your behalf. All human reasoning for hope may indeed be gone, but our Creator is not limited as we human beings are. We always have the option to choose to have faith in His word: "With men *it is* impossible, but not with God; for with God all things are possible" (Mark 10:27 NKJV). Let your faith rise even now to believe He will not permit the one who trusts in Him to lack any good thing (see Psalm 34:8–10). And God will assuredly honor your faith. Your unfailing Helper—for His name's sake—will cause your iron to swim!

Our Education

We know from experience that good fathers want to teach their children and guide them the best way they can through life. Where did this desire come from? From the Creator of fathers, of course, our heavenly Father—who embodies all the best (and much more) that defines good earthly fathering. Therefore, it should not surprise us that God would say to us, "I take great pleasure, My beloved child, in educating you."

We also know from experience that "school" is not always easy—and is even, at times, downright stressful and unpleasant! And yet we can be sure, without a doubt, it is for our benefit in the long run. Our faithful heavenly Father will always have our best interest in mind as He puts us through the many "classes" that He knows (in His perfect wisdom) are necessary for our education. The lessons He sees that you need may be quite different from the lessons He chooses for me. There is something that is wise for us to settle in our hearts, once and for all. It is that the One who created each one of us intentionally unique (for His good purposes for us and through us) knows perfectly well the best way to individually educate, nurture, and develop all our inimitable gifts and potential—in order that we may each fulfill our singular destinies. In other words, friend, there is no wisdom in wasting our time comparing our "classes" with the "classes" of other people!

Instead, let us consider taking into our hand (and into our spirits) a special little truth that can be an invaluable advantage to us as we go through our Father's education process. It is just this one simple little sentence: "This thing is from Me" (1 Kings 12:24 NKJV). If I will allow these five short words to settle down into my inmost being, they can give me comfort and sweet rest when I am weary from life's labor—and its disappointments. In this school of life, when I have to tread rugged, jarring places along my path, these words can smooth the way for me and strengthen me, helping me to persevere. "This thing is from Me." Knowing this brief message comes from the One who says that "he who touches you touches the apple of His eye" (Zechariah 2:8 NKJV), I can rest assured that all that concerns me concerns Him too.

When we are assured we truly are precious in His sight, we can trust Him (and trust He has a plan for our good—and knows what He is doing) through all that He sends our way. Yes, our Father will, in His wisdom and in His love, certainly educate His children. But in every circumstance, no matter how difficult and trying, we can know He is the God of our circumstances. It is He who is in control of them. Even when we may unexpectedly find ourselves amid a turbulent storm, this one little thought has exceptional power to calm our fear—and also to enable us to perceive a silver edge on the threatening clouds. In every class in which we find ourselves, we can focus on these five words—and rely on our Father's infallibly and eternally trustworthy character. Consequently, we can accept that we did not come into the circumstances by chance or accident. Rather, most likely it is the exact place God meant for us to be. "This thing is from Me."

Consider some examples. Suppose you find yourself seemingly locked into a disheartening situation where you are made to feel you are not of any worth at all and you are pushed aside as though wholly insignificant. Or you experience the acute loneliness of never being understood, and you suffer rejection and injustice at the hands of the "in crowd." Oh, that is a hard class! We all may quite naturally wonder what in the world a good Father could be desiring to teach you? And yet, on closer examination of this picture, we may discern through the blur of our empathetic tears that at one time you perhaps prayed to be made more like your Lord Jesus. You may not have consciously intended that your request be in the sense of His attribute of humility, and yet would not a "school" in which lessons in humility are taught be an actual answer to your prayer to be like Him—who described Himself as "meek and lowly in heart" (Matthew 11:29 KJV)? Could not these very people around you be instruments sent from His loving hand to answer your own prayer—and to work out His good and perfect will for you, His deeply treasured child?

Or it may be that you are in dire financial straits—scrimping and budgeting and strenuously working as much as you humanly can but still finding it extremely challenging to get by, even to stay alive. This too is a crucial time to remember these words: "This thing is from Me." Your all-wise Father may be trying to teach you the vital, key principle that He Himself is your Provider—and He wants you to clearly and profoundly comprehend that His supplies are limitless (see Philippians 4:19). He has faith in you that you will pass this test. A formidable trial? A tough, grueling lesson? Absolutely! And yet once learned (as you have become well educated in how to utterly depend on Him), how greatly will you please your Teacher. You will have been blessed with the high privilege of being able to demonstrate and prove to onlookers of your life that your God's promises are faithful and true! Believing God (what He tells us of His goodness and of His utter reliability) and having experienced for yourself that He is worthy of your trust in the face of all appearances to the contrary—what an inestimably valuable class from which to have graduated!

There are indeed many classes in the good Father's school for His children. Consider this: could we ever truly be deeply acquainted with the Son of God, "a Man of sorrows and acquainted with grief" (Isaiah 53:3 NKJV), if we ourselves never pass through classes of sorrow and grief of our own? And even further, perhaps there has been no one on earth who could offer us compassion and consolation during our dark nights. Why would our gracious Teacher allow this added pain? Perhaps, precious sorrowing one, it is that we might turn solely to Him—and come to better know Him (who alone can give His beloved child comfort and peace that is everlasting). Thus, once again we can be helped along the way by His gracious words: "This thing was from Me."

The all-wise One, who loves us immeasurably, knows we have need of "this thing" (whatever the trial may be)—although with our limited vision, we may not be able to see the reason at the present moment. Yet, knowing our Savior Himself has gone before us on every path He takes us down, we may look up into His dear face (even through our tears) and confess to Him our confidence that His grace will indeed be sufficient for us through each trial. As we embrace the essence of these five small words, "This thing is from Me," they can be like an extraordinary lubricant to "grease the wheels" of our ability to accept and handle every challenging circumstance that comes into our lives. If in our loving Father's chosen school for each of us, we learn to see Him at work for our good in everything (both for now and in eternity), that acquired realization can wonderfully temper and assuage the pain of every trial. May we learn well the prized lesson of knowing with all our hearts that His way for His cherished children will always prove to be the best way.

No Road
without Its Springs

There is an old saying: "Trouble never comes to us except she brings a nugget of gold in her hand." As long as we are on our pilgrimage through the years of time while we are on this earth, trouble will be a part of all our lives. One day it won't be so any more, but while we are here, it is.

In ways we may not yet comprehend, living in this land of trouble is a valuable opportunity, for it is only when we are weary that we can learn the sweetness of rest. It is only when our hearts are breaking that we can experience the preciousness of Love healing our aching hearts. And it is only when our souls hunger and thirst that we can know the richness that alone can satisfy our deepest need. God's angels do not know these things but we human beings can.

Perhaps in the end we will not only conclude the lessons were worth it but also thank God for all the ways He chose to bring us. As extreme as it may seem, I believe with all my heart in that day (when the "suffering chapter" in the book of our lives is over forever) we will be able to perceive His loving wisdom in such fullness that if we could, we would not want to change anything in our lives!

And so trouble does come to us. At times our path will take us through desert places—parched places of the burning heat of adversity or the drought of disappointment and apparent waste. At other times, our course will lead through dreary, low places of humiliation, grief, or loneliness. But if I am certain I am in the way of God's commandments, I need not fear when the path of duty turns into the wilderness. His loyal disciples will discover that God has no dry road without its springs. He does not leave us to traverse alone our valley of suffering. All His good promises to His children are unfailing springs. He made a covenant to be a Father to those who covenant with Him to be His people—and God's promises are never revoked. Throughout all human history, His people have found the springs of strength and comfort their God has faithfully provided for them. "As your days, *so shall* your strength *be*" (Deuteronomy 33:25 NKJV).

Every faithful pilgrim will find God has gone before him. Like all good parents, our heavenly Father anticipates His child's needs, and His foresight and love prepare provision. Those who are God's own will be surprised all along the way by His miracles of grace. "He turns a wilderness into pools of water, And dry land into watersprings" (Psalm 107:35 NKJV). Our God can make water gush forth from the rock (see Numbers 20:11), and even in the ruts of the hardest roads, His children will find growing flowers of abundant consolation and lilies of peace.

Significantly, His promised provision for our journey is not like a stagnant pool, but it is as an ever-flowing spring that does not shrink in times of drought. In fact, it is the time of trying drought that most reveals the spring's rich fullness. And it is the hour of my need that confirms the promises to me as sure and certain—and stamps indelibly upon my heart the imprint of His trustworthiness. And thus it was that Paul came to rejoice in his infirmities (weaknesses). How was that possible for him? It was because it was through his weakness and need that he discovered the rich supply of his Father's grace (see 2 Corinthians 12:9–10). The greater our need, the larger the pitcher we can bring—and always fill! "There is a river . . ." (Psalm 46:4). Ah, how precious are its waters for our thirst. And how much more there is to be possessed of our God's fullness!

No, trouble, I will not go looking for you. But inevitably you will find me. When you come to me, though, I will look for the gold nuggets that you bring to me in your hand!

Chapter
42

Inside the
Rough Oyster Shell

I once read of a man living in the late 1800s who sold diamonds. He sometimes had to mail the diamonds to buyers, and when he did, he wrapped the boxes in plain, rough brown paper. He did not want there to be any hint of the valuable items the package contained. I believe our God sometimes sends us costly packages that at first we may not recognize as having any value—because they are wrapped in commonplace, unappealing, or even disagreeably rough exteriors. But in reality, precious gifts of His love, kindness, and wisdom are inconspicuously hidden within.

Oftentimes circumstances that to our natural eyes look unpleasant and repellent, even dark and terrible, can be unwrapped by the trusting eyes of faith in God as assuredly a good God. And we can, by looking deeper, discern their hidden meaning. We may possibly discover that harsh difficulties in our lives can mysteriously turn out to be for our good. The icy sting of winter makes us shiver and moan and long for warm springtime. And yet, the biting cold freezes out pestilence, and the bitter frost breaks up and loosens the soil for the success of future planting. Winter's stormy winds cause the roots of trees to go deeper, providing a better foundation for growth. Thus, we can understand that in many ways wintertime is a "need be." Can we not perceive too that life's worst calamities can potentially provide a better foundation for our growth as well? Perhaps that may hinge on how we receive them.

When trials press in hard against us, it is possible to have many different perspectives on them and reactions toward them. But I have found one of the most consistently productive responses is not asking "Why?" but instead asking "What?" "What, Lord, do You want to teach me through this? Please help me not to miss anything that You, my faithful Teacher, want me to learn." Although my natural man wants to balk at suffering, my spiritual man does want to grow (and produce more yielding to my Father's will in my life). When I elect to not push away the pressing trial, it is then I may discover that it is actually the Potter's hand. When I have chosen to endure its discipline, I have found the pressure (that I had the instinctive tendency to want to resist) was actually purposed to mold my life into a thing of beauty and usefulness.

Among the many treasured jewels of earth, the pearl is the only one drawn from a living creature. And in a sense, significantly, the pearl is an outworking of life overcoming death. A pearl is produced only when the little mollusk living within the oyster shell is wounded. There is one Pearl of great price that is infinitely precious to the Father. It was through the wounding of His own Son, Jesus—for our transgressions— that His life was released to us. Thus, it is much more than a mere principle that treasures can be camouflaged within the rough wrappings of suffering; it is a reality—and it is a secret of inestimable value to discover. In our difficulties, if we cast our cares and anxious thoughts upon such a Savior (trusting that He is working out His good plan—for our benefit), we will assuredly extract from the rough oyster shell of our adversity a rare and priceless pearl.

I Stand with You Against Myself

Part 1

*W*hen we think of spiritual warfare, many targets may come to mind—most of which are "out there." However, in the writings of a godly man who lived long ago in the 1500s, I found these words: "If you want the highest degree of spiritual perfection, you will need to wage constant warfare against yourself."[16] It may be that our greatest, most difficult battles will be against our very selves. (At least, no doubt, that is the best place to start.)

And yet, before I blithely leap into the fight against my own nature, I may be wise to consider that this type of warfare is like no other. I myself am both friend and foe. My own flesh fights against my own spirit. My old man wars against the new man I am in Christ. In this spiritual war, both sides are equal, and the battles will be fierce. To war against my very self will take all the determination, strength, and courage I can muster. To "kill

---

16   Bernard Bangley, compiler, *Near To the Heart of God, Daily Readings from the Spiritual Classics:* "Spiritual Combat" by Lawrence Scupoli (Harold Shaw Publishers, 1998), April 21 reading.

myself" does not, of course, come naturally. Self-preservation is one of the most powerful of human instincts. (Ironically, however, we are not capable of preserving our spirits—and to be negligent of concern for them is the most foolish madness.)

Just as we cannot define *being* or *soul* or *beauty*, we cannot define *self*. We can, however, delineate that *self* designates one person as distinct from another and man as distinct from God. The biblical use of the word seems to specify man as cut off from God (man deliberately acting in defiant independence of Him). The Bible also describes where this *self* was first manifested—and the eternal ramifications of that. Long ago, before the earth and time were, Lucifer, a beautiful and powerful angel created by God, turned into Satan (meaning "adversary") when he chose to rebel against his Creator's authority. Lucifer exalted himself: "*I will* ascend . . ., *I will* exalt my throne above the stars of God; *I will* also sit upon the mount . . .; *I will* ascend above the heights of the clouds, *I will* be like the Most High" (Isaiah 14:12-14 NKJV, author's emphasis). Thus, Lucifer's "*I will*" (that is, his self-will) supplanted submission to God and His will—and the outcome was disastrous.

Satan brought his insubordination to earth and seduced Eve with his notions of rebellious "self." Beginning his strategy by sowing contradiction and confusion about what God said (a principal tactic of Satan's), he then fed Eve self-oriented lies: "For God knows that in the day you eat of it your eyes will be opened, and you will be like God" (Genesis 3:5 NKJV). Satan thus introduced humanity to the lie of self-deification and presumed godhood. Having been taken in by the great deception that they could be their own gods, Adam and Eve rejected God's authority. Their one act of disobedience against the single prohibitive command given to them by God jettisoned them onto the destructive course of self-will and sin. As a consequence, all mankind was separated from God and pursued self (in essence, man's will and way as opposed to God's will and way).

The battle in the Garden of Eden for the control over the souls of mankind did not take God by surprise. He created man with a free will, with the ability to choose—for that was an essential element of being made in His own image. The high and holy purpose of our creation was for a love relationship with our Creator. And love cannot be forced; it is a choice. We choose to love—or not to love. God well knew what the people He lovingly created would choose. Our forefathers Adam and Eve (with whose nature, unavoidably, we all are born) chose to rebel against trusting God's love for them. Like Adam and Eve, we have all used the precious gift from God of our free will to choose to side with self against our Maker. At root, the original sin was created man saying to his Creator, "not Your will, but mine be done." We opted to be in love with ourselves over loving God.

However, in another garden—Gethsemane—the Son of God most solemnly and earnestly demonstrated for fallen mankind the right relationship with our Father: "Not My will, but Yours be done" (Luke 22:42 NKJV). All along—from even before the first human beings were created—God had a plan to redeem us from our self-chosen separation from Him (who is our very life source). In the fullness of time, He sent His own Son to this earth: God the Son became flesh and blood, a man—one of us. The entire life of the man Christ Jesus on earth was one of submission to God, His Father. As the eternal One walked for a brief time among us, He showed us by His complete obedience to His Father that God's will assuredly is good—and that God can be trusted.

And then as the culminating act of His earthly purpose, He sacrificed His own life-blood as the substitutionary payment for the consequences of our guilt and sin (for the sin of every human being who would ever live). Jesus's death in our place (the Just for the unjust) fully satisfied God's righteous justice (that required we deservedly pay a price for our rebellion against Him). Christ's taking upon Himself the debt we owed God our Maker opened a way for us to return to being what we were originally created to be: trusting children of God. In humble childlikeness (instead of the aggressive pride of self-assertion), by relying on what Jesus did on our behalf, we could find our way home to our Father's heart.

Thus, if we choose to put our faith in Jesus (in the reconciliation to the Father that Christ's pouring out His life accomplished for us), then His Holy Spirit will teach us how to follow Him—to be His disciple (one who learns by the example of his teacher to be like his teacher). Jesus taught His followers that they must think differently than other men—learning to think a new way (as He thinks) if they were to follow Him. "If any one desires to be my disciple, let him deny himself—that is, disregard, lose sight of and forget himself and his own interests—and take up his cross and follow Me [cleave steadily to Me, conform wholly to my example in living and if need be in dying, also]. For whoever is bent on saving his [temporal] life [his comfort and security here], shall lose [eternal life]; and whoever loses his life [his comfort and security here] for My sake, shall find [life everlasting]. For what will it profit a man if he gains the whole world and forfeits his life—his [blessed] life in the kingdom of God?" (Matthew 16:24–26).

The more we cling to our self-life and to this mere earthly life, loving its rewards (popularity, power, financial security, ease and pleasure, etc.), the more we will discover how empty these rewards really are—and we will forfeit the best from Christ in both this world and the next. If we will loosen our greedy grasp on the transient things (which are all this world can offer us), we can be set free to follow Christ Jesus. This is one essential characteristic of the "about face" that must occur if we are to truly live (to live eternally, as we were created to). It is part of the necessary transformation from the natural man's thinking to thinking as a spiritually renewed man—to having the mind of Christ (see Philippians 2:5–8). As we embrace this essential transition to be "new men," it will become our deepest desire and wholehearted commitment also to align with Jesus in saying to our heavenly Father, "Not my will, but Yours be done."

Think of it. If we were able to enter the very "Holy of Holies" in Gethsemane and reverently listen to our Savior's awful plea at the prospect of taking our sin onto Himself, "Father, if You are willing (if there be any other way), remove this cup from Me" (Luke 22:42, author's paraphrase), there we may begin to comprehend the price at which our redemption was bought—and we would come to know the real value of things. (Not in Gethsemane can I retain a frivolous or flippant spirit or hold a cheap, "easy" religion.) In the extreme agony of the battle within (fought for our sakes) Jesus sweat drops of blood as in prayer more earnest and intense than we will ever know He surrendered His soul to His Father's will. Then an angel from heaven appeared to Him and strengthened Him in spirit (see verse 43). And, friend, wherever and whenever you or I surrender to the Divine will, an angel of God will come to us and refresh our souls too. We will discover that the laying down of self is the taking up of the infinite God—and that the moment of surrender is also the moment of conquest. I lose my will (and yield up my weakness), and I put on like a robe His strength and majesty. I embark on becoming what I was born to be.

Several facets to this spiritual combat against self should be considered if we want to win in this war. At the epicenter of the war is our choice to love ourselves more than we love God. To understand the nature of our warfare, we must reflect upon what turned us upside down (from submitting to our Creator's will to preferring our own over His). Particularly fateful aspects of our choosing to go our own way (see Isaiah 53:6)—to live independently of God's directives for us—include our presumed self-sufficiency, our decisive rebellion against our Maker, and our lack of trust toward God our Father.

Self-Sufficiency

Notably, and indisputably, Satan himself wants to be worshipped above God (who created him), and it is no wonder he tries to manipulate us into following in his insidious steps— to seek to steal glory from God for ourselves. Satan defrauded Adam and Eve by planting the lie in their minds that they themselves could be "as God"; therefore, they deduced that they did not need God. When the serpent thus deceived them, instead of remembering the goodness of God in giving them life and abundantly providing for them, Adam and Eve were persuaded to swallow the delusion that they could obtain more on their own. The struggle between man's prideful self-sufficiency and his trust in a kind and generous God continues today within the wills of all mankind. This temptation to believe we can be self-sufficient has warped every human being's spirit since that pivotal beginning when the decision of our original parents resulted in their relationship with God being broken.

Theologians use the term *moral depravity* to describe the extent to which our entire human nature has been damaged by the separation of our spirits from God our Maker. This doesn't imply necessarily that each of us is as bad as we potentially could be, but it does mean we are all fallen, broken beings, and flawed spiritually—in that our stubborn inclination is to live for ourselves (self-centeredly) and rely on ourselves rather than accept our dependence on God. The Bible teaches that we were created to be in a relationship of love and submission to our Creator—and we are designed for the privilege of being His servants (in which we would find our highest pleasure). Correspondingly, we would feel empty and unfulfilled if we tried to serve anyone or anything other than God Himself (see Ecclesiastes 12:13).

By blinding the creature to the truth of his dependency on the Creator, Satan may have presumed he had won the battle—but one battle is not the entire war! "I can do it on my own" is a powerful delusion indeed and infects us all. Even so, our God-instilled consciences spur us to the inevitable recognition that we fall short of being and doing as we were born to. Inevitably we find ourselves flinging up our hands with the eternal question, "How? How can I be delivered from this bondage?" Paul described this internal tendency and the failures of his own human nature as a wretched state: "not able to do what I want to (what I unmistakably know is morally right and good) and continually doing what I don't really want to (things that I loathe)" (author's paraphrase, see Romans 7:14–23). Our disastrous mistake is thinking that we are "up to it" to win this warfare by our own efforts—not realizing we are utterly without strength in comparison with our adversary (who capitalizes on our self-will to the advantage of his own malicious rebellion against God). As far as our own strength is concerned, we are actually hopeless to cope with Satan's power. We are no match for him—and we are no match for the instrument he uses, "self." Our enemy is too cunning and too strong for us.

The Bible acknowledges that we love ourselves (see Matthew 2:39; Ephesians 5:28–29) and that there is a right kind of self-respect (valuing our being made in the image of God). Simultaneously, it teaches us the rather disconcerting but necessary truth that we must also hate ourselves (our own lives) (see Luke 14:26–27). It is not that God wants us to hate our big nose, or bad memory, or short legs, or clumsiness, but rather He wants us to despise something far more serious and dangerous to our true and lasting welfare—the self-reliance and self-centeredness of our fallen human nature. Paul's willingness to despise the part of himself that was spiritually faulty and unprofitable can be compared to the wisdom of a builder who recognizes the need to tear down a condemned building before he can build a new house on the same land (or a coach who tears down his players' self-confidence before they can become willing to play his kind of winning ball). Similarly, the Lord finds it necessary to convey that we do not have a reason to feel good about ourselves (indulge in inordinate self-esteem) as long as we are determined to live for ourselves and trust only in ourselves (defiantly refusing dependence on our Maker). Like Paul, we need to hate this tendency—and cry out for deliverance from it (see Romans 14:24–25).

One reason God allows His people to experience trials and difficulties is so they can make us more conscious of our weakness and how we have overestimated our own powers. When huge waves of trouble, poverty, reproach, or sorrow flood over us, we learn the littleness of man—and we are thereby more fitted to learn the majesty and greatness of our God. Often it is by no other means that we will come to self-emptying and be delivered from our foolish presumption and darkness as fallen creatures. The ever smooth and even path is less likely to open our eyes to the revelation of God's lovingkindness and His power to deliver us. Self must get out of the way to make room for God to be rightly exalted in our hearts. Thus, we can be thankful for any road of affliction that God may use to deliver us from ignorance of our weakness and of our need for Him.

When we come to the end of our own strength (when we are emptied of our own self-sufficiency and our own most resolute efforts to keep ourselves from wrongdoing and to overcome self-absorption), we are positioned to receive a very marvelous revelation. On that most significant threshold, we begin to comprehend that our help comes only from Christ Jesus—not from ourselves. And the magnificent reality is that the battle has already been won for us! Through His love for each one of us, which engendered His laying down His life for us (see Galatians 2:20), we are enabled to become more than conquerors over all our enemies. The Captain of our salvation's victory over Satan and his hordes is freely given to us who yield ourselves to that Captain's lordship over our lives.

Paul shared with us his own profound realization of not being self-sufficient and independent (as we all so tenaciously tend to assume we are) in these seemingly incongruous words: "When I am weak, then I am strong" (2 Corinthians 12:10 NKJV). He came to understand that when he yielded his human strength in submission to Jesus as his Lord, then he was paradoxically made strong—in divine strength. The mighty Prince of heaven, the Son of God, was willing to be made weak so we could experience the power of God—and He was willing to be impoverished so we could be enriched (see 2 Corinthians 8:9). The strength of Christ never grows strong in us until we acknowledge and accept that we are weak. (To the degree we retain of our own strength, we lack Christ's.)

The principle for all of us that the Lord disclosed to Paul was that the power of Christ would actually be perfected (completed and show itself most effective) in and through our weaknesses. Thus, the illusion of our autonomy and self-determination could give way to the truth of the power available for us through our being dependent on God! Just as the Son yielded His will to His Father's, as we follow Jesus's lead and yield our wills to our Father also, we will make the inestimably vital discovery of God's truth that "My grace—My favor and loving-kindness, and mercy—are enough for you, [that is, sufficient against any danger and to enable you to bear the trouble manfully]" (2 Corinthians 12:9). His grace—this consummate gift—is enough! When the clay puts itself back into the Potter's hands, that is deliverance—and that is the beginning of restoration!

Rebellion

When Jesus beseeches us to follow Him (in this essential matter of death to self), it is because He knows with absolute certainty that any person who desires to come into God's kingdom must enter by God's own specified door. Jesus Himself is that door; He is God's appointed way. The Father designated that His Son be "the way" for us to follow if we are to be restored into eternal life in God's presence (see John 14:6; Romans 5:10).

Our Lord Jesus Christ Himself, even though part of the Godhead, nevertheless subjected His own will to His Father's (see John 6:38; Mark 14:35–36). This acceptance of the will of God may be perceived as the yoke the Son of Man carried—and that He invites us to bear with Him. In the will of God, He found rest, and He promises that very rest to those who bear the same yoke. Like our Leader, we need not fear to yield to God's authority (to continually seek to live a life wholly harmonized with our Father) for Jesus will not lead us through any darker room than He went through before us. Consider for a moment the yoke on the ox that looks so heavy and burdensome. In reality, it is the yoke that makes light the toil of the plow or laden cart that would otherwise be hard labor. In the yoke of submission to His Father, Jesus found satisfaction and even joy (even when the will of God brought Him rejection, callous ingratitude, and bitter opposition from those He came to bless with His grace). In our turn, if we can submissively say to Jesus Christ, "Master" (determinedly turning our back forever on rebellion against God and longing that His will be ours), then we will discover we are standing in a fully satisfying, holy place. We are at the very door to our Father's heart—our true Home.

In our rebellion against the God who made us (who created us for a love relationship with Him), we chose to take the side of our own glory against His. Our innate pride wants love and honor for ourselves. Each one of us is thus "wired" by the nature we inherited from Adam and Eve, a nature that is acutely prone to rebellion. Having taken the serpent's bait, we strive just as Lucifer did to be above God (see Isaiah 14:12–15). You and I— all human beings—strongly crave to be "somebodies." (We are somehow convinced we are more worthy objects of respect, applause, affection, and approval than God is!) Inevitably, this rebellion precipitates a conflict within us. We feel a powerful, passionate need to be loved and appreciated—and we dare to demand it of other people, as if we were entitled to it. Oh, selfish man! In love with ourselves! (How could we deserve any tenderness or affection—apart from our Maker?) Indeed, all love and glory belong to God alone. Only God is the worthy object of worship. And yet we manipulatively attempt to win our neighbors' hearts to ourselves—craving that they be in awe of and respect us. It is the human echo of Satan's "worship me." It would do us less harm in the end to steal the incense that is glowing on God's altar than to try to capture what belongs only to God!

Oh, what is the way home again for us self-centered, prodigal children? We must take the side of God's glory as opposed to siding with our conceit and vanity. We must cry out, "Oh, my Father, I stand with You against myself!" The apostle Paul wrote, "Let this mind be in you which was also in Christ Jesus" (Philippians 2:5 NKJV). Although Jesus, the Son, was equal with God (essentially one with the Father), He became of no reputation (willingly stripped Himself of all privileges and rightful dignity)—and humbled Himself to become as a man, and even as a servant of men. The sinless Son of God submitted wholly to His Father, obedient even to the extreme of dying (in our place—the Innocent for the guilty) on the cross (see Philippians 2:5–8). Peter also exhorted us to have "the same mind" that Jesus did (see 1 Peter 4:1)—the mind that lived not to please Himself (nor to please men and the world) but solely to please God His Father. We can only enter this mind of Christ when He Himself has been allowed to enter us. When we willingly follow His example and obey His injunction to die to our "self-life" (when the mind of the old Adam that covetously thirsts to be "something" has been condemned and deprived of its rights), then we can receive and welcome the Son of God into the center of our lives—and onto our heart's throne.

In reality, losing fame or reputation, luxury or comfort, money or earthly security, is nothing compared with losing life. It is our very self we must lose—must give up to God. Man's eye is not single; he always has a side glance toward his own honor. This self-love disqualifies him from beholding the glory due to God. We must give up our love of self—even to the point of dying on a cross. We ask, "How can I do that? How can I put myself to death on the cross?" The Lord Jesus died to help us die! He will give courage to the trembling soul, to the soul of little faith. The Holy Spirit whom Jesus sent is willing to renew our minds—teaching us how to deny ourselves (to disregard and even lose sight of our "self" and its own interests). Jesus deserved glory, but He chose sacrifice and pain. He asks us to follow His example, willingly choosing the path of obedience and humility—whatever it may cost us. When we, as Jesus did, offer our lives to the Father (our wills to our Father's will), then we will be gifted with becoming partakers of the very mind of Christ. When we opt to be on His side, not on our own, we can become new creatures—and embark on a new realm of living.

Significantly, however, as long as any secret need to be approved and respected remains in us, we are not yet dead with Christ (and will not be able to enter His resurrected life). The task of "dying" must be diligently pursued. Inevitably, we will experience an ongoing battle within. Still we will struggle, wondering if we will ever cease wanting to impress others—hungering to be popular, applauded, admired. We must become indifferent to these demands of self-love! The errors of the old man must be buried; the old ways of thinking and believing must die. It isn't easy or quick. The old ways of behaving don't vanish at once. Every now and then that which we thought had died springs back to life again! We mutter that we don't deserve certain treatment, and we complain in self-pity, even accusing God of being against us. Yet, if we have truly made the sacrifice complete (when we are no longer of any concern to ourselves), what then can losses or injustices toward us matter?

This dying—this renouncing of self—is a process. As we heartily embrace it, we will think less and less about what happens to us and think more and more about God. His will be done—that is sufficient. To really get down to the business of sacrifice, we must cut every string—and offer our all to God. There is no other way. (And yet, would we really want something other than the will of God? Do we belong to God or to ourselves?) Our prayer must be, "Take my life. Don't let me hesitate! I draw no protective line around anything that needs to go." The watchwords of a soul that is filled with the mind of Christ become "I delight to do Your will, O my God" (Psalm 40:8 NKJV) and "Father, glorify thy name" (John 12:28 KJV).

The wondrous blessing hidden within this self-renouncing life lies in these matchless, eternal verities: he who loses, finds; he who dies, lives; he who humbles himself is exalted (he who humbly gives up his own rights is raised up into the resurrection life of Jesus—and to a divine position of authority); and he who possesses nothing has all things (for whatever we surrender for Christ's sake, we find again—transfigured). Although, indeed, everything must be sacrificed, remarkably and wonderfully it will be returned with interest. What we have lost is compensated for by infinite, eternal gain. When we turn away from the world and "come out from among them" (see 2 Corinthians 6:16–17 NKJV), we will not be left desolate like orphans. The Lord is waiting for us; He Himself receives us! When we have lost all that is in us, we will recover it all in God!

We have lost the whole world and gained the unsearchable riches of Christ.

When His mind has taken possession of us, it gives us an inner contentment with the way God leads us (see Psalm 16:11). Whatever our lot may be—though it be as seemingly insignificant a place as a stable in Bethlehem or the carpenter's home in Nazareth—all worry over our own will and way can come to an end. When we have the mind of Jesus, wherever we are will be transfigured into a place of holy, divine service (because the Father will always be glorified through the mind of the Son).

God came to us in Christ, and the more we are "in Christ," the more our self-love will be transformed—until it becomes like the self-giving love of God. God's agape love is undefeatable benevolence and good will—always seeking the highest good of the person loved. God does not love because He hopes for anything in return, but He loves with agape love, which delights to love and freely gives. God, being love itself, loves because it is His nature to love—whether or not we deserve it. Jesus was the highest expression of this selfless giving of our God—for God's faithful, committed love for us led to the sacrifice of His own Son on the cross for those He loves (see 1 John 4:9–10).

The Word of God exhorts us to be other-directed, not to live for ourselves but to live first for Him who died for us—and then live for others (see 2 Corinthians 5:14–15; Philippians 2:3–4). The example of the selfless Son of God calls us to selflessness—

and away from selfishness. Those who claim to have been crucified with Christ must live for Him first and through Him for all about whom He cares. (The world is full of lonely, weary, and desolate lives to whom Christ would send us as channels of His love if we were ready for His use.) "Even as the Son of man came not to be ministered unto, but to minister, and to give his life a ransom for many" (Matthew 20:28 KJV).

This highest type of love is not based on feelings but is an act of the will—a resolve, with joy, to put the welfare of others before one's own. Agape love does not come naturally to us. Because of our fallen nature, we are incapable of producing such a love. But as our heart's response increasingly is "yes, Father" to the will of this God of love (and we increasingly stand at His disposal in life and action, in doing or letting be, in working, or in suffering), we will be more and more conformed to the image of Jesus—we will become like Him. Consequently, our very love grows to become like the love of Jesus for His Father. "For I have come down from heaven, not to do My own will *and* purpose; but to do the will *and* purpose of Him Who sent Me" (John 6:38). And Christ honors those who honor Him and His Father. By our love for Him, we draw our Beloved. And in responsive communion with our Savior, we find that death opens into life as it should be—as we return to oneness with our Creator.

Lack of Trust

Undoubtedly, the most fundamental element causing mankind's incomparable loss in Eden (and the rudimentary principle within ourselves that we must conquer in order to return to "Eden") is our lack of trust in God. This is the most relentlessly tragic aspect of Satan's theft from us. At the very core, then, our battle began and will end as a fight for God's honor. God's character is utterly and eternally trustworthy. Satan's perpetual lie to us is that God is not trustworthy. We forfeited our strong and intimate connection with God when we chose to not believe Him—but rather to believe His adversary, Satan. We joined with our deadly enemy in maligning God's character. "Because when they knew *and* recognized Him as the God, they did not honor *and* glorify Him as God, or give Him thanks. . . . They exchanged the truth of God for a lie and worshipped and served the creature rather than the Creator" (Romans 1: 21, 25). At rock-bottom, this is the essential question for each of us to answer: Is God trustworthy? (Is He worthy of my utter trust—and thus also my obedience and submission to Him?)

Consider the depth of these holy, unparalleled words: "He who did not withhold *or* spare [even] His own Son but gave Him up for us all, will He not also with Him freely *and* graciously give us all [other] things?" (Romans 8:32). This is the nature and character of our God! He gave up for our sakes His beloved, only-begotten Son so we would know—assuredly and undeniably know—His trustworthy love for us. Let us pause here to thoughtfully note that this unsurpassable and supremely significant act (of God's delivering up His dearly beloved Son) was done for us who had set ourselves against Him as His enemies! "God shows *and* clearly proves His [own] love for us by the fact that while we were still sinners Christ, the Messiah, the Anointed One, died for us. . . . If while we were enemies we were reconciled to God through the death of His

Son, it is much more [certain], now that we are reconciled, that we shall be saved [daily delivered from sin's dominion] through His [resurrection] life" (Romans 5: 8, 10). Why would God do such a thing for the good of His enemies? He did it to win His enemy (what man in his heart had become)—to overcome them with love! This is the act of our God that most lets this enemy see God's love. And most gloriously, it is the act that enables His enemy to truly love again—in the ideal and holy manner that we were created to love!

Jesus's entire purpose in taking on our nature of flesh and blood (and the object of His earthly life from birth to death, His ministry from beginning to end) was an open invitation to a restored connection with God. When Jesus taught His disciples to pray, He was inviting them back into a relationship with God as "our Father." God the Father sent His Son to reconcile us with Himself—from whom our distrust and unbelief had separated us. "But God! So rich is He in His mercy! Because of *and* in order to satisfy the great *and* wonderful *and* intense love with which He loved us, Even when we were dead [slain] by [our own] shortcomings *and* trespasses, He made us alive together in fellowship *and* in union with Christ.—He gave us the very life of Christ Himself, the same new life with which He quickened Him. [For] it is by grace—by His favor and mercy which you did not deserve—that you are saved (delivered from judgment *and* made partakers of Christ's salvation). And He raised us up together with Him and made us sit down together—giving us joint seating with Him—in the heavenly sphere [by virtue of our being] in Christ Jesus, the Messiah, the Anointed One" (Ephesians 2:4–6).

Jesus paid the ultimate price so nothing need ever again separate those from God's love who come to the Father through Him. Just as a father does not despise his children's weakness or need for help, Jesus in no way will cast out or reject anyone who determines to come home to his Father God through Him (see John 6:37). God provided His Son's sinless perfection as the atonement (to make the payment) for the sins of all mankind—so everyone could be welcomed home again. Paul taught this gospel (good news): "I am persuaded beyond doubt—am sure—that neither death, nor life, nor angels, nor principalities, nor things impending *and* threatening, nor things to come, nor powers, Nor height, nor depth, nor anything else in all creation will be able to separate us from the love of God which is in Christ Jesus our Lord" (Romans 8:38–39). What greater indication could there be of the utterly trustworthy love of God toward us than the cross where the Son of God died—in our place? Almighty God was crucified by His own creation! This is indeed "amazing love!" His love and goodwill toward us never has to be in doubt. What God did for us in the person of His Son is the ultimate answer for all our spiritual need.

I Stand with You Against Myself

Part 2

The unshakeable reality of God's trustworthiness does not negate the fact that in our limited human nature we will not necessarily be capable of understanding all our Father's ways with us. "For my thoughts are not your thoughts, neither are your ways my ways, saith the Lord. For as the heavens are higher than the earth, so are my ways higher than your ways, and my thoughts than your thoughts" (Isaiah 55:8–9 KJV). The very nature of our spiritual lives in union with Jesus, though, is that even in our uncertainty we can be certain. We may not be certain of the next step on the path of His will for us, but we are certain of God's character. We can trust our good Father! Jesus, the Son of God, who is "the express image of God" (Hebrews 1:2–3) came to reveal the Father—to make Him clearly known to us (see John 1:18). We can trust this same Jesus, who eternally bears the great name "Faithful and True" (see Revelation 19:11).

It is important also to consider that it is our Lord Jesus who said, "Except ye be converted, and become as little children, ye shall not enter into the kingdom of heaven" (Matthew 18:3 KJV). A little child can live a basically carefree life because even though he himself cannot comprehend certainty about anything else in life, the child is certain regarding his parents. The simplicity of that trusting is enough for the delighted child. When Jesus took such a little one into His arms to instruct the disciples, He was guiding them to understand that humble childlikeness is more aligned with the reality of who we are (dependent creatures, not capable of independence—as we mistakenly assume). A little child cannot know which way to go, nor can he provide for himself, but his loving parents carry him. This is what God does for us. Just as the mother eagle actually carries her fledglings on her back as they are learning to fly (see Deuteronomy 32:11), God's trusting children can rest assured that "underneath *are* the everlasting arms." (Deuteronomy 33:27 NKJV; see Isaiah 46:3–4). God Himself will "spread His wings" beneath us, His cherished children, and will carry us—teaching us to trust Him where we can see no earthly support on which to rest.

Jeremiah accurately expressed our true state: "I know that the ability to determine his own way is not in man himself; it is not in man (even in a strong man or a man at his best) to direct his own steps" (Jeremiah 10 :23, author's paraphrase). This reality is the very reason God's Word teaches us to "lean on, trust *and* be confident in the Lord with all your heart *and* mind, and do not rely on your own insight *or* understanding. In all your ways know, recognize *and* acknowledge Him, and He will direct *and* make straight *and* plain your paths" (Proverbs 3:5–6). In contrast to the proudly aggressive spirit that contends for place and power (which, although it may force many a door, will not find them to be doors into enduring wealth and peace), it is the childlike spirit that finds life's truly golden gates all ajar. Inheritances of real and lasting value become ours only through humility. For "God sets Himself against the proud (the insolent, the overbearing, the disdainful, the presumptuous, the boastful) and opposes, frustrates and defeats them—but gives grace (favor, blessing) to the humble" (1 Peter 5:5).

The Greatest of All made Himself Least of All. God the Son emptied Himself of His majesty and took on the vulnerability and lowliness of an ordinary human baby. How can we (dust and ashes) be haughtily self-important after our God so humbled Himself? Unless we bow our proud heads, we will not be able to get through the lowly door of humility—and we will be unable to enter the kingdom of God. When we perceive and grasp that the very God who made us made Himself a little child for our sakes, how could we still be puffed up, great in our own eyes? We are only leading ourselves astray!

Many people yearn for and willfully pursue worldly recognition, but God has a higher calling for His children. Although the proud may indeed win the applause of the world (and may assume they have succeeded), they have signally failed if all they have is in essence as a shadow—and they have missed the true substance. Thus, the boastfully conceited and insolent are grievously self-deceived, unaware of their own defeat in the eternal realm. In contrast, the lowly have stopped struggling to "be as God"—and know themselves to be but men. The humble people unpretentiously (yet wisely) accept that they are as children dependent on their father.

Israel's greatest king, David, wrote, "Lord, my heart is not haughty, nor my eyes lofty; neither do I exercise myself in matters too great or in things too wonderful for me. Surely I have calmed and quieted my soul, like a weaned child with his mother; like a weaned child is my soul within me [ceased from fretting]" (Psalm 131:1–2). As a bird folds its wings and comes to rest, when we finally learn to "fold our wills" (choosing to steadfastly trust in our loving, good Father rather than in ourselves), we will at last find the rest and genuine security for which our spirits are longing. The heart that trusts God is the heart that will be encompassed by true and sustained peace. "You will guard him *and* keep him in perfect *and* constant peace whose mind [both its inclination and its character] is stayed on You, because he commits himself to You, leans on You, *and* hopes confidently in You" (Isaiah 26:3).

As we continue to explore the nature of this spiritual combat we are called to wage against self, we must recognize that self involves the will. Because of man's inherited sin nature (see Psalm 51:1–5), his will is naturally predisposed toward himself. Notably, self is emphatically not given to submission to anyone—other than itself. All man-initiated religions (from the most legalistic to the most liberal and mystical) have their variations of willful "works salvation," and inevitably self is at the core of their methodologies for attempting to achieve a positive consequence (of some sort or another) regarding life after death. Significantly, however, no self-purification ceremonies or rituals, no self-realization techniques, no psychological self-actualization theories or skills can ever change an individual's sin nature (of rebellion against his

Maker). Self is the vehicle of sin and is thus the very breeding ground of rebellion. Self insists, "Not Thy will, but mine will be done!"

Thus, for everyone who rejects yielding to the sovereignty and authority of the God of the Bible, self (and its schemes to attain godhood) is the only option left—and self becomes the only hope for resolving humanity's plight and problems. The dilemma is that self is mankind's number one problem! If there is to be a genuine solution to humanity's self-oriented, self-willed predicament, then rather than pursuing self-deification, what is paramount for mankind is choosing to accept again submission to his Maker and Owner.

Deliverance from man's quandary must start with a new birth—a spiritual birth from above (effected by God's own Spirit). By receiving (through faith alone) the simple message of Jesus Christ's atonement for our sin (and obeying His teachings found in the Scriptures), a person can be born again spiritually—and with a new spirit become a new creation. Even with a new identity in Christ, however, the believer still retains his old sin nature. The difference is that he has been delivered from the power of its control. "Who gave Himself on our behalf that he might redeem us (purchase our freedom) from all iniquity and purify for Himself a people—to be peculiarly His own—[people who are] eager *and* enthusiastic about [living a life that is good and filled with] beneficial deeds" (Titus 2:14). For the rest of the believer's life on earth, though, battles will continue between following his own self-will and doing God's will. But the good news is God has gifted every believer in Jesus with His Holy Spirit to help him win every battle in favor of his Lord's will. The way of life intended for us that the Son of God demonstrated through His perfect selflessness (see Matthew 20:28; John 15:12–13) would be an example impossible for anyone to follow except for the fact that every believer has been sealed by the Holy Spirit—who enables him to allow the very life of Christ to be lived out in him (see Ephesians 3:16; Galatians 2:20).

As we begin to comprehend and embrace the primary truth that we need a healthy distrust of ourselves and simultaneously need expanding confidence in God, then our being at its very core will become reoriented aright (as our Creator originally intended it to be). The assurance that we can absolutely, positively trust our Father (whether our limited understanding can comprehend all His ways) is a vitally important spiritual weapon. If we hope to be able to increasingly gain victory over the self-life (especially in our minds, where God's adversary constantly tries to infiltrate our thoughts with the lie that God is our enemy), this confidence must be our bedrock. Essentially, we must also remember that it is a fight for our God's honor! (Where will we take our stand: Is God trustworthy or not?)

Also, it is incalculably crucial to realize the significance of determinedly choosing to indeed engage in this spiritual war—for, in reality, we must either fight or die! Unavoidably, our eternal lives are at stake. And once this spiritual combat is begun in earnest, we must never lay down our arms; we must never leave the battleground. Amy Carmichael wrote, "Swords drawn up to the gates of pearl!"[17]

---

17   Amy Carmichael, Gold Cord, *The Story of a Fellowship* (Christian Literature Crusade, 2002).

Thus, if our hearts are set solely on rightly relating to God (on honoring Him with our wholehearted trust)—and if we step out in faith, desiring to obey Him in every area of our lives—we will pray, *Fulfill in me the good pleasure of Your will and the ideals You have taught me to cherish.* Wanting to be "in Christ" (in union with our Savior—whose prayer was "Not my will but Yours be done") and seeking to live in the power of our risen Lord, we will banish forever all thoughts of indulging our flesh (human nature without God). Rather than permitting all God's lavish treasures of grace to be wasted on us, we will instead diligently follow after holiness. We will seek to be holy as He is holy (see 1 Peter 1:15–16) and to be "conformed to the image of His Son" (Romans 8:29 NKJV). We will resolutely fight the fierce battle against self—asking of our Captain the courage to let nothing hold us back from repulsing even the weakest inclinations of self-will.

Like a man who discovers a robber in his home and fights vehemently to resist him, we must unremittingly return blow for blow against our own thoughts that would ally with self against God. Victory over self requires that we battle to subdue appetites, to control passions, to live above worldliness, greed, and the pride of life—and, above all, to become free of the false security characteristic of fallen human nature that presumes we can trust self. Rather than think we can become "good enough" by our own efforts, we dare not forget the vast possibilities of sin. We may rationalize, *I have not committed murder, nor am I guilty of adultery*—while simultaneously not having begun to even identify in ourselves arrogance, deceitfulness, malice, slothfulness, envy, anger, rival loves (idolatries), bitterness, or a thousand other sins!

Perhaps having overcome open sins, we yet must understand that the delusive traps of the satanic hunter abound (and he often stealthily schemes to defeat us in the most secret realms of our soul). "For we do not wrestle against flesh and blood, but against principalities, against powers, against the rulers of the darkness of this age, against spiritual *hosts* of wickedness in the heavenly *places*" (Ephesians 6:12 NKJV). We are compelled to be aware the enemies of our souls are obstinate and fierce and that there is no chance for an arbitrated peace with them. We are encouraged in Scripture to stand firm in our faith in God because it must indeed be "through many hardships *and* tribulations we must enter the kingdom of God" (Acts 14:22). Evil never surrenders its hold on any of us without a sore fight. We will not come to spiritual victory against sin and self by way of the pleasantries of any child's play, but rather on a harshly ruthless battlefield—where freedom will cost us the price of blood. The apostle Paul wrote, "I die daily—that is, I face death every day and die to self" (1 Corinthians 15:31).

In this spiritual warfare, it is necessary that we never excuse ourselves because of our weak human nature. Our God well knows the constitution of our battle and our personal caliber. "As a father loves *and* pities his children, so the Lord loves *and* pities those who fear Him—with reverence, worship and awe. For He knows our frame; He [earnestly] remembers *and* imprints [on His heart] that we are dust" (Psalm 103:13–14). If our strength fails us in battle, we may ask more from the Lord—and He will not refuse our request. (It is our Father Himself who encourages us to engage in spiritual battle, delighting in our choosing to undertake it. Therefore, a victory gained is very pleasing to Him.) If we should ever conclude the struggle is hopeless, then we do God a great injustice. It is true enough that we are no match against self. But any soul that sincerely looks to God is equal to the battle! The only thing the Lord asks of us is that we do fight—doing so courageously. And yet even so, although we may put up a terrific fight against our own lower nature, we can only, as it were, trample down the weeds. Uprooting the weeds is something only God can do. That is why we turn to Jesus! He is the Victorious One (see Colossians 2:14–15) and is the Captain of our salvation. And He it is who fights for us!

This is what the Lord says to you: "Do not be afraid or discouraged by this vast army (the enemies of your soul) for the battle is not yours, but God's" (2 Chronicles 20:15, author's paraphrase). Don't lose heart, good soldier—for as you fight the good fight, you do not fight alone. Even if your enemies are great in number, the love of God that holds you is infinitely greater. Elisha knew the angels of God fighting on the side of His people were much more numerous than the enemies coming against them. And he prayed for the eyes of his fearful servant to be opened to see this reality also (see 2 Kings 6:15–17). The Lord will gladly open our eyes too! Remember Goliath (symbolic of the enemies of God). He seemed to have everything on his side. But all he blusteringly boasted in having actually counted for nothing—because he didn't have God! With God against him, he collapsed at the touch of apparent weakness. (The issue was not David versus Goliath but God versus Goliath. And so it will be with us who are on God's side in this warfare.)

Despite any wounds you may receive, never give up the fight. Sooner or later He will crown you with victory. Our testimony surely will be as certain and triumphant as Paul's was: "I have fought the good (worthy, honorable and noble) fight; I have finished the race; I have kept (firmly held) the faith. (As to what remains,) henceforth there is laid up for me the [victor's] crown of righteousness—for being right with God and doing right—which the Lord, the righteous Judge, will award to me *and* recompense me on that [great] day; and not to me only but also to all those who have loved *and* yearned for *and* welcomed His appearing [His return]" (2 Timothy 4:7–8).

Just what is this thing called "faith" that Paul so fervently fought to keep (that which the devil targets above all else to steal from us)? Faith is the one attitude of a person that is exactly the opposite of trusting one's self. Other human attitudes can somewhat be worked up by our own effort, but faith occurs when we cease trying to do something by our own efforts— and we trust someone else to do it for us.

Salvation (reconciliation to God and restoration to being what we were created to be) cannot be obtained by any effort or merit of our own. God has ordained that it be according to grace (entirely a free gift of God) and that we receive the gift by the heart attitude of faith—of solely trusting in what Jesus did for us. Jesus Himself is the author (the very source of) and the finisher of our faith (the One who perfects it, bringing it to maturity and completeness). And indeed it is He Himself who "for the joy [of obtaining the prize—of *making a way for us to come home to our Father and to return to trusting in Him*] that was set before Him, endured the cross, despising *and* ignoring the shame, and is now seated at the right hand of the throne of God" (Hebrews 12:2, author's paraphrase). Will our Savior bear the cross for us, and we expect our path to be strewn with rose petals—without any suffering? Or is there a cross for us?

"Jesus suffered and died outside the gate (in the place of the city's unclean refuse and filth and where the carcasses of the animal sacrifices for the people's sins were discarded; it was there that our Savior Jesus bore the reproach of the world) in order that He might purify and consecrate the people through (the shedding of) His own blood. Therefore, let us go forth unto Him, outside the camp, bearing (with Him) His reproach" (Hebrews 13:12–13, author's paraphrase). What will we choose—love of self, the way of the world (the godless, God-rejecting system of humankind under the influence of Satan, the prince of this world) or the path of the Lamb of God (who wholly submitted His will to His Father's will)?

Loyalty to Christ means separation. It may bring us human rejection, mockery, and scorn. Yet let us consider Moses, who even centuries before God sent His Son to redeem the world, was gifted to see by faith the immeasurable worth of that joy set before Jesus (the Messiah yet to come)—and who was also able to discern the great riches of sharing Christ's reproach. "By faith Moses, when he had grown to maturity *and* become great, refused to be called the son of Pharaoh's daughter, Because he preferred rather to share the oppression (suffer the hardships) *and* bear the shame of the people of God than to have the fleeting enjoyment of a sinful life. He considered the contempt *and* abuse *and* shame [borne for] the Christ, the Messiah [Who was to come], to be greater wealth than all the treasures of Egypt, for he looked forward *and* away to the reward (recompense). [Motivated] by faith he left Egypt behind him, being unawed *and* undismayed by the wrath of the king; for he never flinched *but* held staunchly to his purpose *and* endured steadfastly as one who gazed on Him Who is invisible" (Hebrews 11:24–27). By faith (simple trust in and complete reliance on God), Moses looked away from himself to the greatness of God—and he made his decisive choice that wherever Christ the Messiah led, he would follow Him.

May we too be faithful to the end—letting nothing hold us back from all Christ paid for us to possess. We need to put our relationship with Jesus above every other relationship and to give up trust in any other thing we have thought of as a source life—or that competes with God for control over our lives (see Luke 14:26–27). Just as a seed must die (cease being a seed) to produce a plant, so we need to bury our confidence in all other hopes before we can find the ultimate blessedness of discovering true life through unmitigated confidence in our God.

Fellow spiritual soldiers, as God's priests, let us defy the world (and its merely temporal and ever-changing values), and as God's kings, let us reign over self. May we be those who will press on where others flee—remaining faithful to follow the way of our Leader Jesus, though all others forsake Him. Let our heart-cry to God our Father ever be, "**I stand with You, against myself!**"

We can indeed run the race set before us (and win in this spiritual combat) by looking away from all that would distract us and instead fixing our gaze upon the holy, glorious majesty of Him who gives us every reason to be confident of overcoming in this battle. There is a rest awaiting us who choose to forsake our own will to take on Christ's yoke—and a peace as our yielded will is enfolded in the matchless security of our God's good and perfect will. "Do not be confirmed to this world—this age, fashioned after and adapted to its external, superficial customs. But be transformed (changed) by the [entire] renewal of your mind—by its new ideals and its new attitude—so that you may prove [for yourselves] what is the good and acceptable and perfect will of God, *even* the thing which is good and acceptable and perfect will of God, *even* the thing which is good and acceptable and perfect [in His sight for you]" (Romans 12:2). And thus our hearts can know even now the deep and enduring satisfaction of putting ourselves into the hands of Him who in life and in death proved His eternally trustworthy love for us.

Will I, in the End,
be Dubbed "Foolish"?

"*From one day to the next,*" *the man had told my husband's friend, "everything was changed.*" The man was from the Ukraine, and he shared from his own personal experience. "*We went to sleep one night with everything fine. We had money in the bank; everything was normal. But the next morning it was all gone.*" As I tried to sleep the night my husband mentioned this account to me, the words seemed etched onto my mind: "*From one day to the next, from one day to the next . . .*" Could it really have been so fast?

In every culture and civilization of the world, people have the ancient memory of the great flood that covered the entire earth. It is written in the Book that until the very day Noah entered the ark, people were eating, drinking, and marrying (engaged in all the typical, normal activities of everyday life)—and then the flood came and took them all away (see Matthew 24:38–39). To them the day came suddenly when everything changed! It happened then; it can happen again. A "suddenly" can surprise us at any moment. The unexpected may startle any of us anytime. When the doctor told your wife, "You have only about six months to live," or when the soldiers with wreaths came to your front door with tragic news of your son, you were stunned. Everything changed—from one day to the next. Even one moment to the next.

While on earth, Jesus performed countless acts of compassion, and He spoke many encouraging, gracious, and gentle words. But at times He was forceful, even vehement, and at times He spoke harsh words. He called some people "fools" (a strongly derogatory term). He used the word in a parable after warning a man about coveting (inordinately desiring more and more possessions). In the parable a rich man's fields yielded him an extremely abundant harvest, so he built bigger barns to store this windfall. Then he said to himself, "Soul, you have many goods laid up for many years; take your ease; eat, drink, *and* be merry" (Luke 12:19 NKJV). There was nothing foolish about storing up the bounty, for we are urged to follow the example of the ants to wisely do so (see Proverbs 6:6–8). So why would God call this man a fool?

What made the man foolish was that he left God out of the picture. "But God said to him, 'Fool! This night your soul will be required of you; then whose will those things be which you have provided?' So *is* he who lays up treasure for himself, and is not rich toward God" (Luke 12:20–21 NKJV). He was called a fool because he failed to realize his life was in God's hands—not in his own.

One definition for *ungodliness* is "life unconscious of God." God is not anywhere present in an ungodly man's thoughts.

His mind (the imagination and intention of all his thinking) is filled with anything but God. Once God destroyed the earth because of ungodliness (see Genesis 6:5–7). The man in this parable Jesus told planned carefully for a comfortable life on earth. He was certain he had things "all sewn up!" What he very unwisely failed to do at all was plan for eternity.

Heaping up treasures on earth is one thing (but pointedly, Jesus taught that those objects are inescapably affected by moths, rust, worms, and thieves). In contrast, Jesus exhorted us that investing in a relationship with God our Father will prove to be truly of the greatest value to us. With that as our heart's desire, we will be storing up precious wealth (beyond comparison with anything on earth) in heaven instead—where our treasure cannot be stolen by any thief nor destroyed by moth or rust (see Matthew 6: 19–21).

Does your outlook on life—and most importantly, your plan for the future—have God in it? If not, friend, turn around while you still can. Who can say when it will be too late? Yes, absolutely, "from one day to the next," everything can change! "The fool has said in his heart, '*There is* no God'" (Psalm 14:1 NKJV). May we not, in the end, be dubbed "foolish."

Over the Smoke
of Battle

Yes, without a doubt, we are in a battle. And yet over the smoke of battle, a gleam of light can be discerned by those with eyes to see. Above the sense of despair, above the apparent defeat, we can see God's promises shining ever. Some of God's children live lives of so much more fullness than others of His children—even though they may be in similar circumstances. What is the difference? Both have His promises. Ah, the difference must lie, then, in their appropriation of the promises. There is a very beneficial art we can learn, if we will. It is that of receiving and putting to use every single bit of the knowledge of our God that is revealed to us.

We can, as it were, lay out all God's attributes on the table before us, pondering His revealed character. And such musing can be like a richly nourishing meal for our souls. We can feast on thoughts of what Jesus has done for us. We may be fed by the very bread of life as we meditate on His incarnation—the

Son of God's incalculably gracious condescension to become one of us. As we reflect on the scenes of our Savior's suffering in Gethsemane and on Calvary (all for our sakes), how our spirits can be quickened better than with blood-red wine! Resting in His assurance to us that He is with us always (and that He is ever interceding for us at the Father's right hand), we may drink in His own peace—that He left us as a legacy, a peace that surpasses our understanding (see John 14:27; Philippians 4:7). And when we contemplate the incomparable gift to us of the gracious Holy Spirit, we can assimilate supernatural nutrition from all manner of enriching spiritual fruit and provision.

If we as God's children learn the secret of taking Him at His word (and trustingly believe He will keep His promises—and therefore we act on them), we will be given all the sustenance and hope our souls could ever need. In hours of weakness, we will be able to draw on our Father's own strength and might. Just as the apostle Paul did, we can discover in our weakness that we can be made strong—by the very power of Christ overlaying us. In times of suffering, we are invited to take hold of His own patience and endurance. When we are misunderstood, even hated, we can commit ourselves into the Father's hands as our Lord Jesus did—and know that He will vindicate us (see 1 Peter 2:23). And even when faced with death itself, we will be enabled to appropriate life and immortality, the source of which is our God's very being. "I am (Myself) the Resurrection and the Life" (John 11:25).

May our eyes be raised above the appearance of things (far above the battle's smoke) to the bright banner of God's promises—and

His faithfulness. Relying on His never-changing character, may each of us fight the good fight to "keep the faith" always—ever guarding our hearts in steadfast trust that our God is good . . . that He loves us . . . and that He is in control!

Trackless

The sea appears to be the most trackless of worlds. No footprints mark trails across its fathomless depths. The sea is the very symbol of mystery. And yet when we travel on a ship across it—although we see no path upon the great expanse of waters, nor any sign of shores to give us our bearings—the captain of the ship has a calm faith that he can find his way across the trackless deep.

Observe the master mariner of the old days. He loosened his cable from the dock and sailed away from the land, marking an unseen path toward a port three thousand miles away. For days, weeks, or even months, he went on—with no land or other friendly sail in sight. However, he had no fear. Why? Because his experience had taught him how to steer as though there were a chalk line drawn across the sea. One morning he found himself exactly opposite the desired haven for which he had been steering. How did he find his way across that trackless space? How did he steer with such amazing accuracy, without sight? He did it by trusting his compass and his instruments—

and by looking up into the sky day and night, obeying the guidance of the heavenly bodies. He fixed his course for sailing not by earthly signs but by heavenly lights.

God is described as able to wade through mighty oceans as a man might ford some tiny stream. The plummetless depths of the watery abyss are as nothing to Him who made them. "Thy way is in the sea, and thy path in the great waters, and thy footsteps are not known" (Psalm 77:19 KJV). Even the sea, in every part of it, is the Lord's highway. He well knows the paths across the most trackless wilds—and equally so across our greatest mysteries. John Henry Jowett wrote, "God is never lost among our mysteries. He knows His way about. When we are bewildered, He sees the road, and He sees the end even from the beginning."[18] Just as we cannot trace His footprints across the sea, it is not given to us always to be able to gauge His reasons for circumstances in our lives or to decipher His great secrets. This mighty God marches through the ages with steps we cannot trace, for as mere human beings we have no measure for computing the standards of His realm.

Assuredly, our God does give us an allotted share of "knowing," but mystery is part of our appointed discipline. He chooses what we need to know and what we don't need to know. One day we will be given to comprehend how our being willing to know only what He chose to reveal kept us within safe boundaries. The path down which He leads us may often seem to lead to utter uncertainty, or even to darkness and disaster, but someday we will understand the bewildering sea has been our friend. Uncertainty is one of His ordained means of growth, developing in our lives the needed fruits of hope and

18   John Henry Jowett, *My Daily Meditation* (Barbour and Company, Inc., 1992), June 11 reading.

faith—teaching us to go forth day by day not knowing but learning to trust Him wholeheartedly. We need the mysterious seas of life, for they prepare us for a deeper assurance. Without the overwhelming experiences (the floods of sorrows that we cannot explain), we would never become robust in our spirits; rather, we would remain weaklings spiritually to the end of our days. Although God does take us out into the deep, His way is in the sea. He knows the destination; He knows the track—and we who look up for His guidance on our way shall arrive!

Captains of ships in the service of a country's navy know what it means to sail under sealed orders. Often before leaving port, the officer will be given a sealed envelope along with orders not to open it until after the vessel has embarked. The instructions are not to be read until a specified time. Many times when the captain opens it, he will find only longitude and latitude coordinates. He understands that only after he has arrived at that particular nautical intersection will he be given further instructions when he radios his commander from that location. The captain is likely to have no idea of his ultimate destination but is required to simply, explicitly, and faithfully follow orders from point to point. He knows somewhere out there are specific appointments set for him by his commander that are important—and he determines not to fail to meet them.

Many centuries ago, a similar assignment was given to a man named Abraham. We can read the account of his life, and if we have "eyes to see, and ears to hear" we will discern it was intended by God to be an example to all of us. A gracious hand beckoned that man to leave all he had known up to that point in his life and follow a call of God to cross a vast desert. Abraham did not know where he was going. But for him, it was enough that he was going with God. "By faith Abraham, when he was called to go out into a place which he should after receive for an inheritance, obeyed; and he went out, not knowing whither he went" (Hebrews 11:8 KJV). As the navy captain must trust that his commander knows what he is doing when he gives his orders, so too Abraham was required to trust his Commander.

The ship captain may have no facts or evidence given to him, but Abraham was at least given glimpses. Something of his destination must have loomed upon his vision, for we are told he looked for a city whose builder and maker was God and that he sought a country—a better country, a heavenly one (see Hebrews 11:10, 14–16). Above all, Abraham had a promise—a promise that if he would obey and go forth, he would be blessed (and would also be a blessing). He could endure all the difficulties of his lot because he chose not to look at the difficulties but to focus on that Promiser who had appointed his course. He was willing to rise and to leave all that was familiar to him for an immense unknown because he was acquainted with that One as the all-wise, invisible, and eternal King—who would certainly vindicate Himself as the Promise-Keeper. Abraham, this father of faith (and our example), was content to sail with sealed orders because he had unwavering confidence in the trustworthiness and wisdom of his Lord High Admiral.

When we have entrusted our lives into the hands of our Maker and our God, we will discover that this is what is required of us. Believing our Admiral has an overall plan for our lives, we must venture forward trustingly on the first step of our appointed journey as He directs—and wait patiently for the specifics to unfold in His chosen timing and way. The children of God can open every "sealed envelope" with untrembling hands (knowing the directions are from our Father). As we are willing to yield up our own agenda and desired trajectory and instead obey Him (even in the face of great uncertainty and unknowns), we will find He is faithful to guide us by opening the way before us—many times in ways we could have never imagined. Launch forth on His track; it will conduct you to the open sea—to His best path for your life! He takes the responsibility to bear you to the goal.

Many of us want to know the way (the whole plan, the detailed itinerary, the exact blueprint) before we are willing to start any enterprise. We are not willing to submit to following God unless the plan makes sense to us. And even more, we try to dictate to Him that we want the journey to be one of lying down "in green pastures" and being led "beside still waters." We concede, "I will go, if such and such is the way the journey will be." But He will not show us a chart of all His purposes concerning us. He will not comfort our distrust of Him. The Almighty God, our Creator, will not be pushed into the position of having to answer to you or to me.

There is a very critical and essential matter each one of us inevitably must settle in our hearts. *Is my will committed to accepting that God is God? Or do I choose to align myself with mankind's ancient quest, like Lucifer's, for ascension to godhood—*

wanting to be my own god (see Isaiah 14:13–14; Genesis 3:5)? Indeed, wisdom, understanding, and enlightenment are all tempting bait. Coveting to understand, to be wise in our own sight (and to have the right to know "why") are not the good, innocent motives that they may seem on the surface. Within such deceptive bait, there is a hidden hook. The hook is the temptation to hang onto our self-will. The most basic question we all must answer is, "Will it be my will, my way—or God's?" I am like my mother Eve when I choose to believe the concept of man's autonomy (when I rationalize that I have the right to govern myself). "So when the woman saw that the tree *was* . . . desirable to make *one* wise, she took of its fruit and ate" (Genesis 3:6 NKJV). Has mankind's history really proven that the enticing seduction "you shall be as gods" is truly wisdom? Or is it, in actuality, merely arrogant—and dangerous— willfulness? Except for the thoughts God chooses to share with us, our yielding to the temptation "to know" (our delving into what He wills to keep in the realm of mystery) is still forbidden fruit.

Of course, we have the prerogative to argue about the sovereignty of God. Indubitably, the greatest minds in history have wrestled with the issue of the sovereignty of God versus the free will of man. However, I think I will choose to look at it in a simple way: accepting the inevitable reality that God has a perspective that we do not have. Instead of bucking like an ornery, untamable horse against letting God be the One in control (rather than myself), I will let God take care of the things we humans cannot possibly fathom—and I will target my efforts toward taking care of my God-given responsibilities.

A tapestry has been used as an illustration many times: our perspective is like looking at the backside of the tapestry, with all its knots, loose strands, and tangles. But if we let Him lead the way for us, someday in eternity God will turn that tapestry around, and we will then perceive the beautiful thing He has woven out of our lives. Then many things we did not understand will be recognized by us as having been purposeful and needful (and for our ultimate best). In that day, we will understand—and appreciate. "Oh, the depth of the riches both of the wisdom and knowledge of God! How unsearchable *are* His judgments and His ways past finding out!" (Romans 11:33 NKJV). As long as we are in human flesh, we cannot fully perceive the thoughts of our Creator's mind. But we can find both rest and security in the truth that the all-wise and all-loving One is He who is in control. And we can trustingly wait for "the turning."

We are not left to take our journey into the unknown without guidance. If we go to God to be guided, He will guide us. As we step out, going forward in trust and contentment in His leading, He will continue showing us the way still farther on. "Neither know we what to do: but our eyes are upon thee" (2 Chronicles 20:12 KJV). Wait on God until He makes His way known—because for our highest good, He wants us to act according to His mind. We, His own dearly loved children, can depend on Him to lead us (in His own time and way). As the good Shepherd, who lay down His life for His sheep, He has pledged Himself to convoy us through deep and dark waters to our fold. Truly, He alone knows the way.

As moves my fragile bark across the
    storm-swept sea.
Great waves beat o'er her side, as north
    wind blows;
Deep in the darkness hid lie threat'ning
    rocks and shoals;
But all of these, and more, my Pilot
    knows.

Sometimes when dark the night, and
    every light gone out,
I wonder to what port my frail ship goes;
Still though the night be long, and
    restless all my hours,
My distant goal, I'm sure, my Pilot knows.

Thomas Curtis Clark[19]

---

19   Mrs. Charles E. Cowman, Streams in the Desert, Volume 1 (Zondervan Publishing House, 1965), July 31 reading.

Fret verses Let

I tend, so easily, to fret. Worrying seems to come naturally to me. And yet, when Jesus asked His followers if worrying could add anything to their height, He was quite pointedly guiding them to consider whether worrying could really accomplish anything (see Luke 12:25). I am learning that it does not. Nothing positive, that is. Because it does produce something. It produces misery. When I fixate on my fear, my obsession rolls over and over in my mind, robbing me of the ability to think of anything else. For the Christian, this should not be. Anxiety torments. And peace, not emotional torment, is the legacy left to us by our Lord Jesus (see John 14:27).

What is it I worry about? What do any of us worry about? Usually, it is matters having to do with this world. The Lord called them *the cares of life*, and He taught His disciples that such can choke out the growth of the seeds of His words of truth that are intended to give us life (life abundant, life to the full). I am a slow learner. However, more significantly, I do want to learn! The wise man of old wrote, "The lot is cast into the lap;

but the whole disposing thereof is of the LORD" (Proverbs 16:33 KJV). If something as simple as the casting of a lot is really guided by the Lord, how much more are the events in the lives of His children? Even circumstances that seem accidental are ordered by Him. "The steps of a *good* man are ordered by the LORD, And He delights in his way. Though he fall, he shall not be utterly cast down; For the LORD upholds *him with* His hand" (Psalm 37:23–24 NKJV).

When I am troubled about things in this world, my thoughts are often basically self-serving. I cannot be anxious in this way and at the same time be serving my Master. I cannot be simultaneously worrying and trusting. Fear and faith cannot live together in the same house; when one enters, the other departs. When I am fearful (dreading something, fainthearted, or apprehensive), I cannot pray in faith. And faith is what pleases God. Trusting Him honors Him. Our doubting (of His care and His promises to us) dishonors Him.

Our great Teacher gave a lengthy discourse to His disciples about not worrying over the necessities for living—because, Jesus stated, we have a Father in heaven who is quite aware of all we need. Jesus exhorted them to consider this: If He remembers even sparrows, do you think He will forget the needs of His own children? Doesn't He who has numbered the very hairs of your head know all about you? He went on to guide their thinking: Instead of fretting about what you think you desperately need, focus on seeking and striving after God's kingdom and His righteousness (His ways of being and doing right)—and all the things you need for your natural life will be provided for you in addition (see Matthew 6:33) Thus, He taught that if we pursue above all else (as our chief aim) to allow God to rule as King in our lives, then He would assuredly show Himself to be our faithful Provider.

It would be wise for me to consider that when I am worrying about the needs of my life in this world, I am actually meddling in my Father's business. Those things I cannot control are His realm, not mine. And while I am thus meddling, I am actually guilty of neglecting my own business. My business is to obey His leading in the areas of my life where I do have control—over responsibilities He has entrusted to me. My Father will certainly take care of His business of providing for His children. His supplies are immeasurably abundant—and they are laid up for you and for me. "Cast (roll over) your burden onto the Lord (release the weight of it to Him—who wants to bear it for you), and He shall sustain you (He shall bear you up, support and uphold you, protect and defend, and wholly provide for you)" (Psalm 55:22, author's paraphrase). I need to attend to obeying—and let God tend to the providing. Which will it be for us? Will we "fret" or will we "let?"

If I will always remember the heart of loving care of my heavenly Father (as well as His absolute omnipotence), that remembrance can bring a holy calm over my mind. His desire is that His children be anxious for nothing—but that we instead trustingly commit all that concerns us into His keeping (see Philippians 4:6–7; Psalm 37:4–5). As His child, if I walk through life in a quiet cheerfulness and courageous patience, I will reflect to onlookers that I have a good Father. In contrast, if I am disquieted and distracted by cares, then I demonstrate distrust of my Father. Is this not then a grievous sin to thus convey to others that He may not be trustworthy? And must it not deeply wound His tenderly loving father-heart?

Although, of course, there is a responsible consideration and carefulness I should have about my lawful duty day by day, there is no need for me to be anxious about tomorrow, nor about the future—for the future is not mine. The future belongs to God. Our times are in His hands (see Psalm 31:15)—and that means they are in good hands (indeed, the best)! I can surely trust Him who has so greatly and matchlessly proven His trustworthiness to us. "He who did not withhold *or* spare [even] His own Son but gave Him up for us all, will He not also with Him freely *and* graciously give us all [other] things?" (Romans 8:32). Our God, who has provided for our greatest need (reconciliation with Him), will without a doubt provide for all our lesser needs.

So I will choose to leave it to God to choose for me what my life holds, whether bitter or sweet, as He pleases. I believe Jesus has a "program" for my future that involves both my highest happiness in Him and His highest glory through me. He has sent the Holy Spirit, the Comforter, to be my guide through this program, step by step—until Christ's perfect ideal for my earthly life is fulfilled. Therefore, really, my only concern is moment by moment to ascertain that I am letting the Spirit of God lead me. I myself do not need to know exactly God's hidden plan for my future. The veil that hides it from me is woven by the God of all mercy. It is enough that He knows and that it is the will of my Lord Jesus. I do not need to fret and worry because my Father knows what is best for me—better than His child ever could know.

Thought's Channels

I recently read a thought-for-the-day on a calendar about how worry and fear are like a thin trickle of water that gradually digs out a channel in our minds. A result of this is that eventually much of our thinking drains into that channel, often without our even being conscious of it.

I found this concept to be a helpful springboard as I felt the need to counsel my teenaged son the other day. Certain patterns of behavior had developed in his life that were not taking him where he really wanted to be going. To the contrary, they were keeping him "spinning his wheels," preventing him from being the kind of young man he really wants to be deep down in his heart.

After leaving the paved road, we drive seven miles on dirt roads to get to where we live out in the country. Rain, snow, and high winds occasionally contribute to the forming of deep ruts where we drive. "Picture a horse and wagon in the old days trying to stay out of those ruts," I challenged my son. "Maybe if the driver can rein in the horses to move along very slowly and gingerly, it's possible," I continued, "but what about when they break into a gallop?"

It's like that with our thoughts. We think if we are careful, we can control them. But when circumstances speed up (or pressures and varied influences pile up), it is much harder to be in control of all our thinking. This is especially true when there are pronounced ruts formed in our minds—from having repeatedly steered our thoughts in a certain direction in the past. Before we know it, we have slipped back into the old pattern we wanted to avoid and into the ingrained habits we had determined to break. Oh, what is the answer?

Re-channeling! I must make a conscious decision to rein in those horses and direct them down an alternate route. I must recognize the ruts for what they are, and I must put the brakes on the harmful patterns of thinking. I am no longer ignorant of where the road I had been on was leading me. And despite it's having appeared so good at first, I have discovered appearances can be deceitful. "There is a way *that seems* right to a man, But its end *is* the way of death" (Proverbs 16:25 NKJV). Now when I become aware of my thoughts beginning to slip into that negative, carved-out channel again, I can choose to "switch off" those thoughts, just the way I do a light switch on the wall. "That would be a significant step in the right direction," I told my son. "But even so, it's not enough."

To re-route a river, there must be a new channel into which it can flow. It is not enough to just empty our mind (as proponents of certain types of meditation suggest is supposedly to our benefit). That can be very dangerous. God designed us as body, mind, and spirit, and if we willfully disconnect our mind from the rest of our personhood, there are spirits of darkness quite eager to "hijack the plane," so to speak—if given the opportunity! No, it is very unwise to leave a vacuum. As the saying goes, "Nature abhors a vacuum." If emptiness of mind or spirit is created, something will rush in to fill it. Absolutely, we do not want to inadvertently invite the enemy of our souls to take control of our minds—for he has one purpose and one purpose only: "to steal, and to kill, and to destroy" (John 10:10 NKJV).

In the heyday of trains in our country, everyone knew what a switchman was. A train could be barreling down its pair of silver tracks, and then the switchman made his maneuver. With one stroke of his arm, he moved a small portion of the tracks in such a way that upon reaching that section, the speeding train would suddenly shoot off from what the onlookers expected was its trajectory—into a completely different direction.

I pray that the Holy Spirit of God will be my switchman! I entreat Him to cause my thoughts to be turned in the direction He knows is best for me. It's not enough for me merely to try to stop my negative thought patterns; I need to channel my thoughts into the ways of God's truth. When anxious thoughts grip my heart, I will ask my God to help me deliberately turn my thinking into the channel of trust and thankfulness (for His love for me—and for His wise and sovereign control over all that concerns me). When my son is tempted to entertain habits of thought that have been unmasked as purposing destruction of all that is good in his life, I plead with the heavenly "switchman" to please put His hand on my son's mind—and help him set his will to re-route his thoughts. I ask Him to turn him away from indulging in the temptation and instead to yield obedience to God, desiring and trusting His good plan for his life (see Jeremiah 29:11).

I am thankful it is my good Father's desire to give us the mind of Christ—more and more—and to increasingly enable us to have His perspective. "For my thoughts are not your thoughts, neither are your ways my ways, saith the LORD. For as the heavens are higher than the earth, so are my ways higher than your ways, and my thoughts than your thoughts" (Isaiah 55:8–9 KJV). We can learn (for if we simply ask Him to, our faithful Teacher will gladly teach us) to channel our thoughts—from the earthly and temporary to the heavenly and eternal (see 2 Corinthians 4:18). Our God will bring us out from the deep ruts of our lower nature's choices onto the high and holy path that our Savior Jesus trod—of desiring "not my will, but thine, be done" (Luke 22:42 KJV). For in this channel flows the blessed life for which we were born.

The Star-Namer

My family lives in a place on this great globe where there is "big sky." For this I am grateful. In the high desert of central New Mexico, our home is nestled up against the foothills of a mountain range behind us, while in the other three directions are wide open spaces for many miles to other mountains and mesas far in the distance. And so at night we have a striking display of stars that I doubt can be rivaled by very many places on earth. Straight above our house, the Milky Way makes its luminous swath across the dark night sky. The rest of the huge expanse is spattered with countless stars—like pinpricks in black velvet through which we glimpse the light of heaven. I can lie in my bed, gaze at the beauty of the stars, and muse. And often when I do, one particular thought returns again and again to me. I hear a quiet question within: *Has any difficulty I've experienced or anything that has happened in my life (or, for that matter, in all the affairs of men or the upheavals of nature anywhere on earth) made the stars fall?*

Of course, the answer is no. They are still where they have always been. They have not moved. Someone is holding them up. And that same One holds me up, His trusting child. "Underneath *are* the everlasting arms" (Deuteronomy 33:27 NKJV). Yes, I have had days, and at times weeks (sometimes stretching into months and even years), when crises seemed very capable of crushing me down forever into the pit of hopelessness. The word *impossible* seemed engraved across my inner eyelids. I could perceive nothing else.

And yet, there were the stars. They had not fallen. Throughout all the centuries of human history—through the painful circumstances, tragedies, suffering, and sadness of each life— God's stars in the sky remain a steadfast reminder that He is in control. He is sustaining the very universe. And He who "hangs the earth on nothing" (Job 26:7 NKJV) by His fathomless, awesome power is absolutely able to take care of His people— and all that concerns them. His sure promise is that "all things work together for good to those who love God, to those who are the called according to *His* purpose" (Romans 8:28 NKJV). We may tend to think, *I just cannot see how He can do that for me.* But our being unable, through our limited understanding, to put together the pieces of the puzzle does not affect the certainty of this eternal fact of our Father's loving, all-wise care.

Do you know God calls every single star by name? "He determines *and* counts the number of the stars; He calls them all by their names" (Psalm 147:4). Yes, He is that big—and that great! All the vast shining multitude of stars and suns and planets He made and He rules. We have heard how shepherds know their sheep. A shepherd may have a flock of a hundred or more, and yet each sheep and lamb is an individual to him, known in detail. Many a shepherd will have a name for each one of his charges. If our God names the stars (which are, after all, only things—just great masses of matter), how much more does He take intricate note of every person—the cherished, sentient beings whom He made, redeemed, and loves?

This glorious, pre-eminent Star-Namer is at the same time the supreme Healer of broken hearts. These two amazing qualities blend in this one awesomely great and most gracious Being. In the Bible, directly preceding the words describing God as the One who names the stars, is this statement: "He heals the brokenhearted And binds up their wounds" (Psalm 147:3 NKJV). The very measure of His might and strength is the gauge of His tender mercy and compassion. Stars are one thing. The hearts of His beloved children are another. Would He have names for the one and no care for the other? Look at Jesus, the Son of God. It is written that through Him, God made the worlds (see John 1:3). And all through the ages, it is also He who has bent over wounded hearts to heal them. And it is the nail-pierced hand of Jesus Christ that has wiped away tears and silenced sobs with exquisite, divine sensitivity.

There are two places where God says He dwells. He has two temples. "For thus says the high and lofty One Who inhabits eternity, Whose name is Holy: I dwell in the high and holy place, with him also who is of a thoroughly penitent and humble spirit, to revive the spirit of the humble, and to revive the heart of the thoroughly penitent—bruised with sorrow for sin" (Isaiah 57:15). From the unimaginable multitudes of the starry heavens (all at His command), swifter than light, our God of Love comes to hold in His hand a broken heart and heal it. "The Lord is close to those who are of a broken heart, and saves such as are crushed with sorrow" (Psalm 34:18). From star to heart. This God who weighs all the worlds in His hand counts a soul in need of healing far more precious. He will never cease to tend and comfort His own.

Better to Trust in
the Certain –
or the Uncertain?

or the most part, we human beings tend to look to riches to supply our needs—to money (and what we call "financial security") to provide for us the life we can enjoy. But Jesus taught that the man who merely laid up treasure for himself would have been much better off if he had been "rich toward God" (Luke 12:21 NKJV). It would be to his much greater benefit to be rich in a relationship of trust with our heavenly Father. God is the maker of all things, and the statement that He owns the cattle on a thousand hills (see Pslam 50:10) is just a small glimpse into His incalculable resources and ability to provide for His children.

Earthly riches, at best, are uncertain. Paul counseled Timothy to teach others not to "trust in uncertain riches but in the living God" (1 Timothy 6:17 NKJV). Increasingly, we live in times when we may gain money one day and wake up the next day and find a sudden change in the economy has made us poor.

But God is not uncertain, and His character never changes. He is the same yesterday, today, and forever.

We think if we could have a storeroom full of silver and gold, we could secure ourselves against all possible need and care. And yet, the Word of God warns that those who trust in money may be pierced through with many sorrows (see 1 Timothy 6:10). It is because they have built their house on a foundation of shifting sands. And when the rains of difficulties come, they can be caught up in a swirling maelstrom which may drown their very souls in miserable perishing. They trusted in something uncertain.

Our God is a good Father who takes pleasure in giving to His children. The only true place of rest and security for us is in our heavenly Father's hand. Choosing to trust in Him is building our house on the rock that cannot be moved. May we let go our tenacious clinging to things that are worthless in the light of eternity. It is better beyond all comparison to drop securely into His everlasting arms! "And my God shall supply all your need according to His riches in glory by Christ Jesus" (Philippians 4:19 NKJV).

As we embrace the reality of our genuine security being in our Father's faithful and loving care, we can increasingly become freed from a plethora of snares relating to avarice and greed, covetousness and materialism. We will begin to look away from our self-centered concerns and remember we cannot live alone on this earth—no one of us can be entirely independent of other people. As an individual, I am indeed a "center," but part of my life's circumference is every man, woman, and child with whom I come in contact. And we all have "neighbors" (people whose path we cross who need help)—neighbors in the sense of Jesus's parable of the good Samaritan. Actually, a significant part of our new-found freedom will come as we begin using our wealth to minister blessing to others.

Simultaneously, we ought to also consider that a gift of money is not at all the only means of helping our neighbor (that needy person in our circle experiencing any kind of distress). What men and women need most is compassion—and often the kind of help that is hands-on —and above all, "heart-help." Indeed, it may be we are like Peter and John of old, who said, "Silver and gold I do not have." However, if we can also say as they did, "But what I do have I give you (see Acts 3:6–8 NKJV)" and, knowing for ourselves the Lord Jesus Christ (and His absolute authority over all things), extend the power in His name (nature and character) through our hand to that hurting person, we, like Peter and John, may see many a lame man walk. In fact, many people who have had to confess that "silver and gold have I none" have been some of the greatest benefactors of the human race. Remember, above all, that Jesus (the Son of God, equal with the Father) emptied Himself—of all His heavenly status, privileges, majesty, and riches—and became poor for our sakes (see 2 Corinthians 8:9; Philippians 2:4–8). By this matchless, holy act (coming down to our earth not to be ministered to, but to minister), He helped us in our greatest need—as He never could have if He had chosen to remain rich. May He always be our example.

And may we ask Him to show us this very day one of His "little ones" to whom He would have us give a cup of water in His name (for His sake)—letting His love shown to us flow through us (see Matthew 10:42). Trusting in the love of our Father God and the certainty of His faithful provision for us, His children, may we become lovers and givers—like Him!

Tiny Flies

A man once said, "God is great in great things, but very great in little things." Many people think God is interested only in big things and does not want to be bothered with our small concerns. Actually, all we have to do is observe a father and his child to learn otherwise—especially as we realize a good man's father-heart is a reflection of our heavenly Father's heart.

Let's think a moment about a king. Not just anyone can have access to a king. Most people would hesitate to try to approach him. But not so the king's own child. He can even climb right up on the king's lap and whisper into the king's ears, asking all sorts of favors. If it is something his father knows is good for him, the king's child will quite likely get what he asks for!

If we have truly given ourselves to God—having repented of our sin against Him in His holiness—and we are born again (having now new hearts and a different spirit), then we are His dear children. This fact is the basis of, and the secret to, the privilege of prayer. We believe that, like that king's little son, we have been given the right to come to Him in prayer. As His cherished children, we also are assured He as our Father wants us to come—with all our cares and burdens, questions and confusions, needs and wishes, everything. His beloved children can be assured that nothing that concerns us or interests us is too small for Him to be interested in.

A story is told of mountain climbers in the Swiss Alps. Upon reaching a peak, they stood admiring the sublime view. One man in their party was a scientist who took out a portable microscope and, putting a fly he had caught there on the mountaintop under the glass, he showed his friends something very interesting. Although household flies in the valleys below had naked legs, this little fellow had legs thickly covered with hair. The great Creator cared enough even about something as insignificant as a tiny fly to give it little socks!

Yes, the same God who made the majestic, towering mountains cares about the comfort of even the tiniest creatures He has created! And this compassionate God is our God. He who made the mighty, flaming heavenly bodies just as attentively made the tiniest insect—delicately fashioned the lenses of its eye, painted the colors of its fragile wings, and, yes, provided for all its needs. He is interested in "the little" just as much as in the great and awe-inspiring. To such a God, we can bring everything in prayer. Our loving Father is so interested in His children that He is willing to take each one by the hand and care for every detail of his life. To Him, there are no little things. The God of the infinite is also the God of the infinitesimal! He will surely take care of you.

Victorious Spring

*A lthough in winter we may look out upon the barrenness
of the landscape and hear outside the doleful sound of
the wind stirring dead leaves on the ground, we need not
be disheartened.* We can resist borrowing the bleak lines in
that outer world, allowing them to color our heart views,
and instead guard in our hearts a sure sense of the presence
of God. Being assured He is near (and despite how things
appear, knowing that He is even now at work for our good),
we can be glad.

Although the cold and frost seem to hold the earth in an iron
fist, assuredly spring is on the way. The frozen streams and
rivers soon will be broken free from their icy bonds, yielding to
the irresistible power of spring's warmth. In spring, life pours
itself through myriad channels—and year after marching year,
life faithfully shows itself stronger than death.

When it seems evil has triumphed over good, or when the joy of life has fled, take heart. Spring is the harbinger of hope. Just as during the cold, gripping days of winter we can listen deep within us for the sweet minstrel of the coming springtime, we also can choose to cultivate in our pining spirits an illimitable hope. So reach out, dear friend, for a consciousness of the tender love flowing to you even this very moment from God, your good Father. More certainly than the verity that spring is victorious over winter is the eternal truth that good shall prove to be victorious over evil—and joy over sorrow.

And Suddenly
a Light

The apostle Paul was a very intense man. At one point he was intensely, even fiercely, against God's people. Although he presumed he was nobly defending God's cause in persecuting these followers of Jesus, he was drastically misinformed about the truth. In ignorance, Saul's intensity and zeal for God was tragically misdirected.

Then a day came when Saul had a Damascus Road experience. "Now as he traveled on, he came near to Damascus, and suddenly a light from heaven flashed around him, And he fell to the ground. Then he heard a voice saying to him, Saul, Saul, why are you persecuting Me—harassing, troubling and molesting Me? And Saul said, Who are You, Lord? And He said, I am Jesus, Whom you are persecuting" (Acts 9:3–5). "And suddenly a light." Saul's encounter with that Light changed his point of view radically—and it profoundly redirected his impassioned earnestness. And so it may happen with some of us.

God is the one who had intentionally made Saul (who later became known as Paul) such an intense person. He made him to be avidly intense so that one day he would be keenly and ardently passionate for God's purposes and for God's people. He has made some of us, as well, intense and forceful. Perhaps you know someone who is very intense—highly focused and even fiery and vehement about that to which he is devoted. And yet, you may discern his vigorous enthusiasm is presently being channeled in directions that are against God's highest will. Some people we love very much may not be aware that they may be quite intensely going down a detrimental, hurtful, and regretfully destructive road.

God purposefully created that person intense, impassioned. Perhaps He did it to make a Saul into a Paul (to make him too a channel for His blessing to many people). God does not waste anything. Somehow, despite the rampaging errors our free will may have made in our lives, He can find a way in His sovereign wisdom to use the injurious devastation resulting from our misdirected energy and intensity—just as He did with Paul. Our mighty, all-wise God is able to convert even grievous wreckage into miraculous salvage and tremendous blessing—not only for ourselves but also for other lives through us.

As in the case of the prodigal son when he had come to his senses, we too may experience, by God's mercy, our own experience comparable to Saul's: "suddenly a light." And perhaps afterward, we too will make a wondrous discovery—that our regrettable failures can actually help us love God more. For it is certain that at such a junction in life, it will, no doubt, be easier for us to clearly realize we are sinners. Then our need for a Savior will become powerfully serious to our enlightened spirits. The price (of giving His own life) the Son of God paid so we could be acquitted from the consequences of our sin will suddenly overwhelm us—and, like Saul, we will no longer want to live as we had before. For Jesus emphatically taught that a person who realizes he is forgiven much will love Him much (see Luke 7:47). Although this relationship (of the recognized depth of our sin relative to our capacity to love God) may seem to be a sad paradox or lamentable irony, it nevertheless is a deep and significant spiritual truth.

In my own personal life, I recognize that I fell ruinously low before the Lord Jesus lifted me up—by bringing His gracious light to me on my own Damascus Road. Now I can pray, "Lord, You allowed Saul to go very low (and Peter, and others too). With them, I thank you for that 'sudden light' that came to me—and changed everything. What You did for me, in Your matchless mercy and tender lovingkindness, you are willing to do for any other person. Please channel the intensities in us aright, O Lord—that our lives may eagerly, gratefully, and wholeheartedly fulfill Your good, high, and holy purposes."

Ambassadors

*A*n ambassador is a representative of a ruling authority. It is expected that the people chosen by the ruler as his ambassadors would precisely and emphatically represent his own desires, opinions, purposes, and values—exactly as he himself would express them when dealing with other people. They would speak accurately for him, with utmost loyalty to his interests. To do so they would, of course, have to know him very well, and the best and most trusted ambassadors would know the person they represented extremely intimately— mind, soul, and heart.

This is what you and I are called to be: ambassadors. We who have been reconciled to God (restored to His favor, being brought back into harmony with Him) through Christ's atoning death for our sakes are then made "ambassadors of Jesus Christ." In 2 Corinthians 5, Paul taught the Corinthians, "So we are Christ's ambassadors, God making His appeal as it were through us. We [as Christ's personal representatives] beg you for His sake to lay hold of the divine favor [now offered you] *and* be reconciled to God" (verse 20). Paul explained that those of us who have chosen to gratefully receive this marvelous reconciliation to God (provided for us through the sacrifice of His own Son, Jesus Christ) were given, in turn, the "ministry of reconciliation" (verse 18). That is, we are called to aim at (by our words and deeds) bringing others also into harmony again with their God. In other words, we are reconciled in order to reconcile!

For every one of us, having been separated and alienated from our Maker because of our sin (our sin-nature of rebellion against Him) needed someone to bridge the impassable gulf back to our home in His heart. And God our Father wanted us home! So much so that "It was God (personally present) in Christ, reconciling *and* restoring the world to favor with Himself, not counting up *and* holding against [men] their trespasses [but cancelling them]" (verse 19). Our reconciliation was possible, however, in only one way: by "the great exchange." "For our sake He made Christ [virtually] to be sin Who knew no sin, so that in *and* through Him we might become [endued with, viewed as in and examples of] the righteousness of God— what we ought to be, approved and acceptable and in right relationship with Him, by His goodness" (verse 21).

This love of Christ Jesus (His awesomely amazing love for us that motivated God the Son Himself to die in our place) constrains and urges us no longer to live for ourselves— but instead for Him who died for us (see verses 14–15). That unfathomable love essentially should impel us in such a way that we desire no other option but to live wholly for Him. And this loving Savior, who now graciously lives in us (because we have welcomed Him now to rule as King in our reconciled hearts), has given us something vitally important to do for Him: the ministry of reconciliation. He has committed to us the commission to give to others the word of reconciliation—the message of Christ's making the way for us all to be able to come back into favor with our God (verses 18–19). We are Christ's ambassadors (representing the great yearnings of His own heart), commissioned to tell the sin-weary in our world of "the great exchange." We have been entrusted with the precious honor and exceptional privilege of announcing the glad, glad news to hearts searching for true peace—that the way has been made open for them to be reconciled to their Father. They can come home!

As Bread to God

"The fellowship of His sufferings" in which the apostle Paul longed to partake (see Philippians 3:10) no doubt has many aspects. I would like to speak of one aspect that is close to my heart. It is not the suffering of Jesus while He walked this earth. Rather, it is the present suffering in the heart of God—His aching and longing for us.

One may say, "Surely the Omnipotent does not need us!" And that is true. And yet perhaps a higher truth is that He wants us. And because He has of His own free will and choice thus positioned Himself, so to speak, it occurs that when we are not in relationship with Him as He desires, He misses us.

God created us in His image. Every human being who has ever lived was created by God. Whether or not an individual believes he was created by God does not change the fact. We all bear His image—every one of us does. That is why every human life is so immeasurably valuable—every single one.

There is no question the image of our Father in us has been marred. We do not reflect His fair ideal as Adam once did— for awhile. In many, many members of the human race, the beautiful image of our Creator we were born to reflect has been so terribly twisted and warped that indeed it is hardly recognizable. Nevertheless, beneath the layers and layers that may hide it, the stamp is there.

Our Father yearns to see a family likeness in us. He craves to see us be what we were born to be. Many a father or mother can understand this desire. We were created to be like Him. For only those who are alike, whose hearts are in alignment, can truly fellowship and commune. His heart calls to our hearts. Our home is in His heart, and we are restless until we discover that— and in an inexplicable way, He is, too. I've heard it said there is a place in His heart that has my name on it. No one else can fill that place, no one; it's for me alone. He waits for me. He waits for you, longs for you. No one can take your place in our Father's heart.

Sometimes I feel a heavy weight on my spirit. I experience waves of grief. I find myself crying and often groaning deeply within, and I cannot name the reason. Gradually I have come to see it is something very holy that my Father is sharing with me. It is His own grief. It is far beyond my cries for myself, for my own needs. It is in a whole different sphere. I catch a tiny glimpse of His heart, His hurt, His suffering—longsuffering— as He waits for us, the people he created for Himself, to "come around," to forsake our stubborn, willful running from Him, and instead return to Him. He sees us hurt ourselves in our rebellion, in our insistence on going our own way without Him instead of walking on His wise path for us. And just as it affects us human parents with wayward children whose choices are destroying them, it breaks His heart—only infinitely more so.

Yes, we have hunger—hunger for God. But it may be that we have never thought about the hunger of God for us. If we ever entered, even a little, into the sorrow of God over humanity, we have entered a truly sacred place. Perhaps you will be one of the few who desires to enter the very heart of God and feel what He feels and be drawn into the supremely blessed place of sharing His suffering. If the yearnings of His heart become yours, you will never again be the same.

The Love of God

"The love of God is greater far than tongue or pen can ever tell,
It goes beyond the farthest star and reaches to the lowest hell.
The guilty pair, bowed down with care, God gave His Son to win;
His erring child He reconciled and pardoned from his sin.

When years of time shall pass away and earthly thrones and kingdoms fall,
When men who here refuse to pray, on rocks and hills and mountains call,
God's love, so sure, shall still endure, all measureless and strong:
Redeeming grace to Adam's race - the saints' and angels' song.

Could we with ink the ocean fill and were the skies of parchment made,
Were every stalk on earth a quill and ev'ry man a scribe by trade,
To write the love of God above would drain the ocean dry;
Nor could the scroll contain the whole though stretched from sky to sky.

O love of God, how rich and pure!
How measureless and strong!
It shall forevermore endure -
The saints' and angels' song."

Frederick M. Lehman, 1868-1953

(Third verse adapted from a poem written in A.D.1050
by Rabbi Meir Ben Isaac Nehorai)